THE DECISIVE TESTIMONY

MARY BAXTER

THE
DECISIVE
TESTIMONY

Originally published as part of
THE LIGHT AND THE GATE

RAYNOR C. JOHNSON
M.A. (Oxon), Ph.D., D.Sc. (Lond.)

PELEGRIN TRUST
in association with
PILGRIM BOOKS
TASBURGH · NORWICH · ENGLAND

First published 1964
by Hodder & Stoughton Ltd.
as part of *The Light and The Gate*
This edition 1988

© Raynor C. Johnson 1964

British Library Cataloguing in Publication Data

Johnson, Raynor C.
The decisive testimony.
1. Australia. Pratt, Ambrose
I. Title   II. Pratt, Ambrose. (Spirit)
III. Cummins, Geraldine
994.04'092'4

ISBN 0–946259–29–1

Printed in Great Britain
at the University Printing House, Oxford
by David Stanford
Printer to the University

FOREWORD

The first half of this book is devoted to an account of Ambrose Pratt's colourful and surprising life. He was a highly unusual man of keen intellect and massive integrity who occupied important roles both in the East and West.

Raynor Johnson enjoyed a close relationship with him over many years, gradually gaining a keen insight into his mind and character. He then determined to see if he could trace Ambrose Pratt after his death.

The second half of the book records the messages received by Geraldine Cummins, the best of all writing mediums. By their depth of answer to his questions these messages finally convinced Dr Johnson that he now had veridical personal evidence that his friend had indeed survived death with his questing mind and philosophical insight intact. This formed a spiritual watershed in Dr Johnson's own life and no reader can fail to be impressed by the remarkable exchanges of thought which it records.

Ambrose Pratt

Soon after arriving with my wife and family to take up an appointment in Melbourne in 1934, I met Ambrose Pratt at the home of a mutual friend who had invited a few of us to celebrate his birthday.

Ambrose was an impressive figure in any gathering. If a stranger had entered the room where we sat at dinner he would probably have noticed his distinguished appearance and wondered who he was. He was intriguing alike because of his friendly composure and the subtle air of serenity and confidence which he had about him. In social relations he showed a natural old-fashioned courtesy: he would sometimes greet a lady by kissing her hand and bowing slightly, where most of us would use the conventional handshake. The stranger, if of a romantic mind, might have speculated that perhaps he was a diplomat of the old school, or even a man of mystery. Indeed, as I discovered when I got to know him better, the stranger's intuition would not have been too wide of the mark.

I remember an occasion during the war when I had visited him at his home. We were chatting together after lunch when a dispatch rider drove up on a motor-cycle and handed in a message. He told me afterwards that he was combing Australia for a dozen Chinese with qualifications for a hazardous enterprise. They had to be men familiar with a particular type of jungle country. They must be men of courage, resource and intelligence, they must be able to live off the land and able to fade when necessary into the landscape. He was in touch with the Defence authorities, and when these men were found, they were to be given a special training and landed by submarine in what was then enemy-occupied territory, in order to destroy certain oil installations.

I recall him writing in June, 1942 to the Hon. John Curtin, then Prime Minister, urging upon him that the aerial defence of Melbourne against possible attack would be most effectively supplemented by the construction of aerodromes under certain favourably placed hills on Phillip Island. He knew all the relevant facts, both strategic and geological.

Such schemes as these were typical of many which were constantly arising in his fertile mind. Unlike most men, however, a good idea was with him a stimulus to do such things as might help to realise the scheme. If it was outside his range he would give a little luncheon party and press it most persuasively upon those who were in a position to realise it. If it was within his range he set to work quietly to achieve it. The enterprise necessary to translate thought into action was one of his most distinguishing characteristics. "When you come to my time of life", he said, "you will realise how few men have constructive imagination, and how few men are not content with things as they are." I recall a mutual friend once saying to me, "What an important thing it is that Ambrose is a good man."

If the stranger had been introduced to Ambrose Pratt he would have observed a long and well-shaped head, from which the hair had long since gone save over the temples and the back of the head. He would have noted the broad forehead, the distinguished moustache with its characteristically happy upward twirl at the ends, and the trim little goatee beard of the chin. The eyes he would have looked into were brown, tranquil, and benevolent. They contained in a strange way, a sense of unusual insight into character, and an ability quickly to evaluate human nature, as though what they had assessed at once further acquaintance could only amplify. There was more to this than appeared on the surface, and he had some interesting psychical powers of which I shall mention one in passing. He made no secret to me of a faculty which he had possessed as far back into childhood as he could remember, of seeing an aura surrounding the human form (also around some animals and trees). He considered the human aura to be partly a quasi-physical luminescence, the nature of which changed considerably with the condition of health of the individual. He could apparently see the aura surrounding a person's head better against some backgrounds than others, and I sometimes noticed that he might glance at me from a convenient position, and say a few seconds later, "You're looking very well tonight." The faintness or brilliance, transparency or opacity, conveyed to him definite impressions. He told me that in some cases where he had known a particular disease was present, he had noticed associated changes in the aura, and he had no doubt that he could diagnose such a condition in a stranger. He recognised, however, that the human aura embodied elements which were affected by emotional and intellectual activity. He said that in discussion or argument he frequently desisted or changed the subject if he recognised from another's aura that anger or

4

annoyance was developing. I remember that he expressed a desire to meet an American woman psychiatrist who was visiting Melbourne as a lecturer. He remarked about her unusually fine and extensive "golden" aura, and when he discovered that she practised certain meditative disciplines, he said, "Ah! that accounts for it." The three of us made a few investigations of the form of the aura as mood and thinking changed, and also on the ability of the aura to pass through certain physical screens, but we did not do enough to justify any conclusions. I mention this particular example of his psychic faculty in passing, and I cannot doubt that it gave him a certain advantage in his assessment of human nature.

I think I was first attracted to him by an intuition that he had explored more deeply in the region of ultimate things than any of my friends or acquaintances. My own interests were beginning to move at this time from physics to certain wider fields, and the sense that I had met an experienced explorer attracted me and led to a friendship in spite of the difference of some twenty-six years in our ages. In this domain I had the happy privilege of always being the listener and so I gleaned some of his wisdom. My wife and I enjoyed many an hour with him at his fireside, watching him with leisurely deliberation take a cigarette from a little box on a table next to his favourite chair, put it in a cigarette-holder (which he always used), light it, and begin to talk of some past experience or some new idea. In this friendly atmosphere, with a little column of blue smoke ascending from the end of his cigarette, talking quietly and always on some interesting theme, he looked like a mysterious traveller among the elemental things of a timeless world, who had strayed back again into ordinary existence. The riddles of life had always fascinated him, and we were eager listeners.

ANCESTRY

His grandfather and father appeared to have been rather unusual persons, and Ambrose told me something about them. The old Devonshire family to which Henry Pratt (his grandfather) belonged had been closely identified with the professions of law and medicine. They had a good deal of wealth distributed among them. At one time they had owned St Catherine's Dock as part of the family estate. When this was sold, the part to which Henry Pratt was entitled passed into Chancery and was eventually forfeited to the Crown, owing to the delay (over twenty-five years) in making any claim. However negligent he may have been where financial matters were concerned, Henry Pratt had conspicuous gifts of another kind. While a comparatively young man he became a very fashionable London physician. He married the Hon. Harriet Agatha Mytton Lethbridge, but this marriage was not an unqualified success. She was a woman of beauty and distinction, but of so jealous and possessive a disposition that she resented his absence from her side even in the ordinary discharge of his professional duties. At length her jealousy became the source of scandalous gossip and Henry Pratt's patience gave out. Following a bitter quarrel he abandoned the practise of his profession, left his wife and went abroad. Intellectually he was one of the ablest men of his time. Apart from his medical qualifications he was an outstanding linguist and scholar. He wrote a number of books, one of which was on astronomy. He was an expert in Hebrew and Sanskrit, and had a working knowledge of several Oriental languages including Tibetan, Hindustani and Arabic. He had a deep interest in oriental studies and had devoted study to the esoteric side of several Eastern religions. Freed from the life of London he now travelled extensively in Asia, and some of his English friends believed that he graduated as a lama in one of the inner circles of priestly Buddhism. He was known to have travelled in India and Tibet: he remained away for prolonged periods, making occasional return trips to England. Some twenty-five years of his life were spent as a wandering scholar. His deeper interests were in the nature of the human psyche and the field of astronomy. Some of his friends believed that his purpose in paying extended visits to Tibet was to acquire a thorough understanding of the Tibetan science of astronomy which he once declared was greatly superior to the European system. It may be assumed also that he gained a great deal of knowledge of the powers of the human mind the existence of which the Western world is now just beginning to recognise. What he learned he wrote in a number of journals which he guarded carefully, and which after his death passed into the possession of a lady who had been a lifelong friend, to whom he left all his effects. When he finished his travels he retired with her to Bath and became a recluse.

Ambrose Pratt knew of these journals, and when visiting England as a young man, he wrote to this lady, asking her if, as a writer and journalist he could possibly have some literary memento of his dis-distinguished grandfather, hoping by these means to secure these journals, or at least be allowed to see them. She communicated with him through her Welsh solicitor, a Mr Edington, and it was evident that she desired no contact with him. The solicitor who had old-fashioned ideas of family loyalty was distressed at this, journeyed up to London to meet Ambrose and expressed the view that she was not quite normal in her outlook. Mr Edington admitted that he knew of the existence of the journals, and he had understood from Dr Henry Pratt that it was his wish they should pass eventually into the possession of his family. The Will however, constituted everything the property of this lady and nothing further could be done in the matter. Her unusual bitterness was probably to be traced to the fact that she was an earl's daughter and had been subject to scandal and social ostracism because of her long friendship with Dr Henry Pratt. The journals were never traced. It is a matter for speculation why Henry Pratt, who had written a number of books in his earlier years, and who was perhaps not entirely free from the vanity of authorship, should have failed to publish what he had learned in the researches of half a life-time. One would supppose that he could have revealed much of value to mankind, if some intuition had not restrained him from doing so. It is hardly likely that a man of his brilliant gifts and scholarship would have devoted himself for forty years to a fruitless quest. It is probable that he recorded such knowledge as could be written down in the journals, in the hope that some day it would fall into the right hands. If so Destiny defeated his purpose.

There were two sons of Dr Henry Pratt's marriage. The younger son Lethbridge was a naval lieutenant and was killed when fighting in the China War under General Gordon. The older son Eustace was born in 1842. Dr Henry Pratt's strange life had thrown the responsibility for educating his two sons entirely upon his wife who lived at Newton Abbot in Devonshire. He made no contribution to their upbringing, and naturally enough, so strange a father whom they never met was neither understood nor appreciated by them. Eustace chose to qualify in medicine and was a student and later a house surgeon at Guy's Hospital.

In one of the interludes between his travels Dr Henry Pratt paid a visit to his son Eustace and asked him if there was anything he could do for him. Eustace lost his temper and said, "I have never been able to understand the foolishness which led you to throw up a practice of many thousands a year to write a lot of rubbishy books." The older man, offended, took his departure abruptly, and this breach was never healed. As Henry Pratt passed out through the entrance hall he did an extraordinary thing: he removed from a peg his son's overcoat and walked away with it. It was rather an unusual coat, and an expensive one, having been given to Eustace by his mother to celebrate his medical graduation. Eustace never forgave his father for this act. What was his motive? To regard it as mere impulsive theft is to attribute an unthinkable motive to such a man. To regard it as an act by which he sought to punish his son for his rudeness leaves much unexplained, for the act would certainly remain unjustified. Is it conceivable that this extraordinary man foresaw an event which was to happen twenty years later (in 1882), and considered that the coat would provide his son with the most convincing evidence of the part which his father would play in it?

I relate the facts precisely as Ambrose passed them on to me. Henry Pratt lived as a recluse in Bath, Somerset, in his later years. Apparently he never lost interest in his son Eustace as is clearly shown by an incident which made a great impression upon the eight-year-old mind of his grandson Ambrose. Dr Eustace Pratt was at this time a country physician practising in Tamworth, New South Wales, where he lived with his family. Occasionally he was called out to attend a patient in some distant village or township, and this happened one night. Dr Pratt, knowing a boy's enthusiasm for adventure, woke Ambrose up and asked him if he would like to come. Together they harnessed the horse and buggy and drove through the silent streets of the little town. The doctor pulled up outside the shop of the local chemist before proceeding, as he was anxious to get some medical supplies. The chemist awakened in response to their call and said he would be down in a minute. Within a short time a lamp was lit, the door of the shop opened, and a beam of light shone some distance across the darkened street. As the doctor descended from the buggy to go into the shop, Ambrose noticed that he was joined by another person of rather striking build and appearance, who was wearing a broad-brimmed hat and an impressive dark coat with a large fur collar. To Ambrose's surprise, he noticed his father and the stranger engage in earnest conversation for a time. Finally his father walked into the chemist's shop, and the impressive stranger walked over towards the buggy, looked at the boy and said, "So you're Ambrose, are you?" He gazed a little longer and then walked away into the night. A minute or so later, Dr. Eustace Pratt hurried out of the shop, came across to the buggy, and said with excitement, "Where has my father gone?" Ambrose said that he had walked away down the street. The buggy was turned round and an attempt was made to find him, but there was no trace of him. Subsequent enquiries were made by Dr Pratt at the local railway station and hotels, but there was no evidence of any stranger answering to his description having arrived or left.

On the way to the distant patient, Dr Pratt informed Ambrose that the stranger was his own father (Dr Henry Pratt), and that he had endeavoured to persuade him not to make the journey to Nundle that night. He then became strangely silent during the rest of the long drive, but expressed particular annoyance that his father had worn an overcoat which he had himself lost twenty years before under strange circumstances. This detail seemed to astonish him more than meeting his father in a Tamworth street at midnight.

When they reached the village they were met by a man who said, "You'd better be careful, doctor. Mrs Ogier is dead, and Ogier declares he will shoot you. He says if you'd come earlier his wife would not have died." On arriving at the house Dr Pratt went inside and Ambrose heard a shot fired. By a thousand-to-one chance the bullet flattened itself against a medallion which the doctor carried in his waistcoat pocket, and apart from bruising and shock, he suffered no further disability.

The sequel to this sensational midnight adventure followed some five or six months later, when a packet arrived from England bearing the Bath postmark. It was addressed to Dr Eustace Pratt, and when opened was found to contain a full-length photograph of Henry Pratt dressed exactly as Ambrose had seen him. No letter accompanied it, but the photo was inscribed with the date on which he had encountered his son and grandson in the main street of Tamworth. Ambrose had of course never seen his grandfather, but on being shown the photograph by his father, at once recognised it as that of the stranger who had spoken to him as he sat in the buggy on the night of the adventure.

After leaving Guy's Hospital Dr Eustace Pratt joined a friend and they sailed together round the world at a time when this was a particularly adventurous undertaking. Sometime later he joined the Army as a surgeon and was for a time stationed in India. Later he joined the Consular service and was stationed at one of the Treaty Ports on the China coast. His deteriorating health made necessary a return to England. Upon medical advice he then came out to Australia, where it was believed the climate would benefit his health. A stay which was to have been for a few months lengthened into a lifetime. In Australia he met and married Caroline Kershaw. The Kershaws were a branch of an old Yorkshire wool manufacturing family, but Caroline's father joined the military forces and came out as Captain with his regiment to Australia. He subsequently joined the police force and became a superintendent of police at Goulburn, N.S.W.

Dr Eustace Pratt began his country practice at Tamworth, a little town of two or three thousand people. He later practised at Lismore and built up a substantial reputation, being particularly interested in the surgical treatment of cancer. He practised for a time as a consultant surgeon in Macquarie Street, Sydney, but when at one period his financial position was adversely affected by a bank crash, he returned to general practice in Lismore. He was a man of much wider interests than his professional ones. He had a great admiration for the Chinese people and spoke Mandarin fluently. He was also a keen amateur naturalist and made a large collection of animals and birds. In appearance he was tall and distinguished-looking: in temperament he was shy and reserved. To his colleagues he seemed to be rather a stern, silent, unsmiling figure, and some may have thought there was an element of snobbery in his make-up. The truth was that he hated snobbery, but his reserved nature made it difficult for him to make easy contacts with his equals. Dr Pratt and his wife had a family consisting of four sons and three daughters: of these, Ambrose born in 1874, was the third child. He was brought up and tended by a Chinese amah, the widow of an old retainer of his father. Perhaps he owed to this early influence, as well as to the views of his father, an unusual understanding of, and a great admiration for the Chinese people.

YOUTH

When old enough he was sent to school at St Ignatius College, Riverview. Later he went for a short time to Sydney Grammar School. It was at the age of twelve, before the more serious years of his education began, that an event happened in his life which gave him an outlook that no formal education could have provided. One day, he had been made responsible for his little sister, and he had allowed her to drop off the balcony on to the ground below. Even as a boy Ambrose had a vivid imagination and he pictured himself as being tried in court and even hanged for this heinous "crime". Impulsively he gathered a few things together and ran away from home. It was eighteen months before he returned.

Dr Pratt had engaged tutors to teach his children from their earliest years, not only French and German, but the arts of riding, boxing, wrestling, fencing, shooting and swimming. Although still very youthful, Ambrose was not ill-equipped to look after himself. He made his way to a schooner at Broadwater which did miscellaneous trading among the South Sea islands, and he persuaded the skipper to accept him as a member of the crew (with the duties of dish-washer). After this voyage he and another boy went to North Queensland where there lived an acquaintance of his family named Goodwin. He was a drover and adventurer preparing to take a herd of cattle across the continent to the north-west coast. Ambrose joined this party as a "general hand" and thus he came to know a good deal of the life of the "out-back" at an early age. In the eighties of last century, long before the era of the plane, the jeep and radio, those who undertook the continental crossing took risks and were liable to have many adventures.

Half a century later Ambrose told me some of his outstanding recollections of those early days. He mentioned as an outstanding impression, the miracle of the immortelles – the everlasting flowers which carpet some of the plateaux in central Australia.

"We would generally get up in the semi-darkness, the fire would be made and the billy boiled. Then we would saddle-up. I often went in advance of the main party blazing a trail and keeping an eye open for water. Sometimes we might be as much as two days' journey ahead of the main herd. Riding along after breakfast with the sky brightening, there would come the moment when the sun rose above the horizon and cast long quivering shadows hundreds of yards ahead. It is a strange feeling riding over some of these extensive plains. One feels like a poor insect on a huge plate, with the blue bowl of the sky shutting one in. But as the sun rises over the horizon the desert plain becomes, with startling suddenness, a living carpet of lambent gold. The immortelles, under the influence of light, rapidly expand and turn their faces to the rising sun. This quaint prim little flower, which through the night is closed and bent, turns like a worshipper to meet its god. I have known many bushmen who have seen this spectacle as they travelled west across the plains and I have not known any who were indifferent to it.

"Some of the naturally occurring phenomena of the Inland have to be seen to be believed. Occasionally one would pass dry quicksands, a wall of sand slowly moving under the influence of the wind, quite capable of sucking under both men and beasts who ventured too near.

Sometimes one crossed huge dry sandy river-beds strewn with boulders, looking as though water had not flowed there for years. Occasionally water would rise up apparently out of the sand, flow along for a distance, and then disappear once more into the sand.

"No traveller in the Centre can ever forget the monotonous gibber plains, so hard on the horse's feet. 'Gibber' is of course the aboriginal word for 'stone', and there is no hope of finding water in these stony wastes. Water is one of the cattle-drover's dominant thoughts, and the rider's eyes are always subconsciously on the look-out for trees, which mean that water is probably not far away. While the tablelands are well-grassed in good seasons, some of the great interior plains have lost most of their top-soil by erosion, and are covered by little more than drought-resisting weeds with occasional areas of spinifex. These tufts of spinifex have spike-like leaves and may rise as much as two or three feet above the plain. They have no great value as fodder, but seem to be Nature's attempt to provide something living in order to hold the top-soil from complete dispersal.

"The tint of the country sometimes becomes blue-grey, due to the different species of salt-bush. From a distance, these patches may even look like a crop in some civilised area. There are many varieties of salt-bush, and most of them are splendid for cattle food, but large areas covered with salt-bush always contain a proportion of poisonous shrubs. Some of these have a curious property of driving cattle who eat them mad, before they kill them. The drover needs a good deal of skill and experience in avoiding bad country and finding a good route with sufficient pasture. There is a great thrill in this, for over hundreds of miles the drover is pitting his wits and good judgment against relentless Nature, and if he makes a wrong decision the results may be fatal.

"On one occasion I remember that we came to a very bad area, a desolate plain which the horses were obliged to circumvent. Very foolishly, accompanied by an aboriginal boy, I decided to take what I thought would be a short-cut, and go directly across one of these. It proved far more extensive than we thought. Our supplies ran out, and at the end of three days we were struggling across the plain without either food or water. Fortunately the rest of the party got anxious about us and some of those who had circumvented this area came back to meet us and helped us through. It had been foolish of us to make this attempt at a direct crossing, as we had no means of making a fire and employing smoke signals.

12

"One strange memory of the lonely bushman whom one occasionally meets in these outlying places, is his taciturnity. He has an amazing absence of curiosity. He may have met no other human being for weeks, yet if he meets you, he may ask a few questions about a neighbour's cattle, or he may admire your horse, but he is not interested in you – why you are there, or where you have come from.

"The aborigines' method of smoke signalling is always amazing to the white man. By its aid, the movements of strangers, or of horses and cattle, become known hundreds of miles away perhaps even weeks before it is possible to verify the information given. They use grass which is damped with water, so that it emits thin dense columns of smoke. Then, with pieces of bark which they manipulate skilfully, they are able to make the smoke column assume strange forms which, in clear air, convey information to a great distance. It is possible that some communication is by what we call telepathy, but I think this is mostly within the tribe itself.

"It is quite a mistake to imagine that the aboriginal is illiterate. He undoubtedly has some primitive form of written language. He scores wood-bark and sticks, and messages are sometimes conveyed by hand in this way. In later years, when I was once travelling in the Inland, I met an interesting German Egyptologist who had been living for some time with aboriginal tribes in order to study their language. I remember spending a whole night talking to him in his tent, and he showed me some of his treasures. He assured me that the Australian aborigine had a pictographic language of his own."

Ambrose Pratt arrived back home after eighteen months of wandering. He had written to his father and mother, but it is not surprising that these communications had not been received and that they had heard nothing from him during the whole of this time. His little sister, who had unwittingly been the cause of his leaving home had suffered no serious injury. His father left him in no doubt of his stern disapproval of the boy's conduct: time, however, effected a normal restoration of family relationships.

There followed after this, the less romantic atmosphere of school life, for which Dr Pratt's foresight had laid a sound foundation. As a student at Sydney Grammar School Ambrose caught the attention of the Head Master, Mr Weigall, because of his unusual memory and ability. About this time a bank crash in which much of Dr Pratt's savings were lost compelled him to withdraw from consultant practice

F

13

in Sydney and return to Lismore. He wrote to the Head Master informing him that he would be obliged to withdraw Ambrose from the school. Mr Weigall then wrote to Dr Pratt asking that he should be allowed to be responsible for the education of Ambrose until such time as Dr Pratt's financial position was different. The offer was generous and meant with the kindliest of intentions, but it hurt Dr Pratt's pride, and for a considerable time he was unwilling to disclose the offer to his son. Eventually he did so and left the decision to the boy. Ambrose thought it over and said to his father, "I should be disinclined to owe my education to anyone in the world except yourself." The decision was one which his father must have hoped for, and from that time forward a new affection and understanding grew between them, replacing the estrangement which Ambrose's adventurous youth had created.

Originally it had been intended that he should follow his father's profession, but this being now impossible, he was articled to a friend of his father who was a solicitor practising law in Tamworth. This gentleman who had private means and very little practice, kept his office open more for prestige reasons than for business. He connived at a good deal of absence on the part of Ambrose from the office – a fact which his father did not discover until long afterwards. About a year before the young man's final examinations were due, the solicitor's conscience must have pricked him, for he had a serious talk with Ambrose and convinced him that if he did not work hard and pass he would have wasted several years of his life. Ambrose had not done any serious study during this period: he had indulged in many eccentricities of behaviour and had enjoyed a good deal of social life. The solicitor blamed himself, and after a serious talk, arranged for Ambrose to be transferred to the Sydney office of the Hon. W. E. V. Robinson, advising the young man to work very hard so as to pass his examinations and also acquire a sound knowledge of legal practice. The advice was taken in time. Ambrose passed with distinction and then set up in practice on his own account.

He found in himself a growing interest in politics, and became increasingly sympathetic with the ideas and outlook of the new-born Labour Party. He engaged a great deal in political debating, and with a natural ability to speak well, made the acquaintance, and later enjoyed the friendship of W. M. Hughes, J. C. Watson, and W. Holman. He wrote a good deal at this time for the infant Labour Press at the office of *The Australian Worker*. The maturing processes of his thought were probably influenced by some of his father's friends who were brilliant men and took a personal interest in him. Among these were Henry Levien, Sir Henry Parkes, Sir George Dibbs, B. R. Wise, Sir Edmund Barton, J. F. Archibald, W. Macleod, T. Saunders, the Hon. J. B. Nash and Kenneth Mackay. Some of them would have liked Ambrose to enter political life under their aegis, but his sympathies were pro-Labour and he felt a tension between his personal views and the feelings of friendship and respect which he entertained for several of these older men who he knew would be deeply hurt if he pursued a political career in opposition.

He was twenty-one at this time: qualified to practise law, but without any marked enthusiasm for doing so.

The spirit of adventure was still in his blood – perhaps a legacy from his grandfather. He gave in to it, and joined, as a managing clerk, a party of traders who owned a sailing-ship and were engaged in the South Seas trade in copra, pearls and pearl-shell. Disputes which arose from time to time with the native crew were generally referred by the captain to Ambrose Pratt, who appeared to have had an unusual sympathy and understanding of native peoples, so that he was trusted by them. It was on one of these trading runs that a little adroit persuasion on the part of the managing clerk convinced the captain that a call at Apia might be worth while from a trading point of view. Through this, Ambrose had a memorable meeting with Robert Louis Stevenson. He described it to me as follows:

"One of the ship's mates and I went on shore to deal with one of the traders on the island. While we were in his store, an altercation took place between this trader and a customer. Apparently by chance there came into the store a remarkable looking man. He was tall, lean, stooped and thin, with a long face and dark hair brushed back: but I remember especially his eyes which at times lit up with a strange quality of illumination, as if they were lighted from within. He intervened in the dispute, quickly adjusted the difference which had arisen, and as he turned round, I said to him, 'You are Mr Stevenson, I think?' He said 'Yes, how do you know?'

" 'Well, I have read all your books, and I think I should have formed a good idea of what their author looked like. I think your *Catriona* is the sweetest love-story in the English language.'

"I suppose no author can hear his books praised by a youthful hero-worshipper without being attracted to him. At any rate he asked

15

me to return with him to his home Vailima which was a few miles away. I spent only one night there as our vessel left next morning. I do not remember clearly any other members of his household, except in a shadowy way, his son-in-law Lloyd Osbourne. My interest was of course focussed on Robert Louis Stevenson himself. I referred during the evening to a poem of his which had been published in a Sydney periodical. I recall that he then produced a poem which he had just written, and gave it to me. I had confounded cheek in those days, and I remember telling him that I wished he would spend his energy on prose rather than verse."

Ambrose Pratt returned to Sydney at the age of twenty-two with the idea of beginning practice again. For a short time he did so, but in the following year his father died at the early age of fifty-five. It was supposed by his family that he was in comparatively comfortable circumstances, but this did not prove to be the case. After some fretting, his widow mastered the new situation and threw herself into the training of the growing members of the family of which Ambrose was the eldest at home. This made the more urgent a decision as to his life's work, and Ambrose finally decided that he would abandon law with which he was becoming increasingly dissatisfied, and take a risk with writing and journalism which had long appealed to him and in which he had some grounds for thinking he could make money. With this decision taken he shortly afterwards sailed for England.

JOURNALISM AND WRITING

Those who seek to philosophise about human life are constantly faced with the inter-relationships of what appear to be pattern, freedom, and chance happenings. The trifling, and apparently chance happening, seems to be again and again a turning-point upon which important events depend. Knowing that Ambrose Pratt was visiting England, a friend who was a wholesale jeweller in Melbourne, asked him to purchase on his behalf fifty Rotherham lever gold watches. These particular time-keepers were renowned for their reliability and quality. They were made by an old-established British firm, and the standard wholesale price was £20. A credit of £1,000 had been forwarded to Ambrose Pratt's account in London by the jeweller. On arrival there, Ambrose wrote to the firm of Rotherham, placed the order, enclosed his cheque, and asked that the watches be packed and exported. Within a few days he was surprised to find his cheque

16

returned with a polite note that they regretted their inability to comply with the request. Realising that he had perhaps made a tactical error through inexperience, he got a banker's cheque and forwarded it again with a renewal of the request. The next day a member of the firm of Rotherham called personally at his hotel to convey an explanation of their inability to meet his request. It was a tradition of their firm not to deal with new customers. They accordingly limited their output to a certain number of watches per year. Ambrose expressed his astonishment at this extraordinary state of affairs, and asked if they would take exception to his giving some publicity to the view that this was an unduly conservative policy for British trade and commerce. No objection was raised, and he wrote a letter to the *Daily Mail*. Almost immediately afterwards he left for the Continent and travelled extensively there. A series of telegrams signed Alfred Harmsworth pursued him on his travels, asking him to call and see the latter at his office. On returning to London he did so, introducing himself as the writer of the letter. It seemed that the reproach he had levelled against English manufacturers had given rise to an enormous volume of letters to the newspapers most of which indicated that they were no supporters of a limited output. It was in this way that Ambrose Pratt first came to meet Alfred Harmsworth, afterwards Lord Northcliffe, the Napoleon of the British Press. Northcliffe quickly recognised in the young man who had caused his office to be flooded with letters to the Editor a potentially successful journalist, and offered him a position on his staff. The overture was declined, but on a later occasion Northcliffe offered him an open contract which involved Pratt in no specific obligations, leaving him free to travel to any part of the world and write as and when he pleased, but arranging for liberal remuneration for any articles supplied. As this offer did not bind him to hard and fast staff responsibilities, Ambrose accepted it, and did in fact travel widely and write for the paper. Northcliffe's anxiety to attach Ambrose Pratt to his paper was partly due to the publication of two novels, *King of the Rocks* and *Franks: Duellist* which had been immediately successful and run into scores of cheap editions.

A young man arriving in London with a career to make can find himself very lonely. Ambrose was fortunate in that his flair for writing soon opened doors in Fleet Street for him. Among homes where he was received with cordiality and friendship were those of T. P. O'Connor and Sir Francis Burnand (then Editor of *Punch*). He became in due course one of a little group of writers whose short stories were to be found in the popular magazines of that time: *Blackwood's, The Nineteenth Century, The Strand*, etc. Short story writing was a remunerative activity. It led to his tasting the sophisticated social life of London of that time but he found it worthless and let it go. He made many friends in London especially among sculptors and painters. Gilbert, he knew well, and Bertram Mackennel. Arthur Streeton and George Lambert were both there gaining increasing recognition. Ambrose saw a great deal of the world through his travels in Northcliffe's service. He had published several novels, and the leading magazines were happy to pay generously for his short stories. He began to be attracted again by the thought of Australia, and in 1905 made the decision to return. He still continued to send articles to the *Daily Mail*, interpreting Australia to Britain. Most of the outstanding figures of the Federation era were portrayed in this way, and several of these articles led to personal friendship between the author and subject. The time came when Ambrose felt he had written himself "dry" for the Northcliffe Press, and he wrote returning one of the cheques, and indicating this feeling. Northcliffe returned it to him and would not hear of his resignation. This game of shuttlecock continued until Northcliffe realised that it was useless to continue. What, however, led to some anger and bitterness on Northcliffe's part was that when they were discussing the continuance of his engagement, Ambrose Pratt had written in one letter that he no longer cared to write articles of a trashy character as he desired to become a journalist in the best sense and write articles which would influence public opinion. To Ambrose Pratt's sorrow, he realised too late that he had greatly wounded Northcliffe, for what he had written reflected upon the latter's discrimination as an Editor. Northcliffe never forgave him.

There was an interesting sequel to this some years afterwards. Northcliffe was making a visit to Melbourne, and knowing of this, Ambrose wrote him a friendly letter of welcome. A secretary whom Northcliffe had engaged to deal with his correspondence, afterwards told Ambrose how Northcliffe had torn up this particular letter with some violence, and had refused to answer it. His pride would not allow him to recognise defeat at any point, and it was difficult to forgive an employee for voluntarily retiring from his service. He was generous to those who served him, but asked from them the last ounce of effort.

This is perhaps an appropriate place to make reference to the published work of Ambrose Pratt. It covers a variety of fields. Two dozen of the books are novels; there are two critical appreciations of other countries, Malaya and South Africa; two are popular books written about the Australian lyre bird and the koala; four were concerned with economic and commercial subjects; in addition, there is a little biography, belles lettres, and three plays. To this must be added several hundreds of short stories buried in by-gone magazines of England and America, apart from newspaper articles. The works of fiction were all written between the ages of twenty-five and forty-two, solely, as he confessed with an apologetic air, to entertain the public and secure an income. They are compounded of melodrama, of wild and exciting events, of plot and conspiracy and swift-moving action with a dash of romance. The formula was designed to appeal to a wide public, and Ambrose called them pot-boilers. His heroes and heroines alternated between passion and misunderstanding when they were not caught up in the net of sensational events. Certainly they were the products of an extraordinary imagination which all his friends recognised. Frank Fox (afterwards Sir Frank), who was in early years a collaborator, confessed that he was fascinated by Ambrose's capacity for weaving fantastic yarns. He said, "We would walk down the street and have lunch together, Ambrose recounting some adventure all the way. As we sat down in the atmosphere of this, I thought to myself, 'He'll order half a lion for certain'. But when the waitress came Ambrose smiled angelically, and begged for a lamb cutlet."

He told me that some of these books, first published at a few shillings, often ended in paper covers at threepence on the cheap bookstalls of the world where they sold in hundreds of thousands. From some of these enormous circulations he derived no royalties, as he had not safeguarded his interests.

In 1935 after a long interval, Ambrose Pratt wrote a novel called *Lift Up Your Eyes* of a type very different to its early predecessors. Its characters are normal people of the present day, and the book is primarily concerned with character study, ideals, religious views and a philosophy of life. In Peter Gaunt, who is the principal character, idealism burns strongly, and the discontent, aimlessness, unhappiness and materialism of mankind oppress him. He plans to reform the world but realises that this task belongs to "the flaming zeal, the radiant energy, the lustrous single-minded faith of unspoiled youth". Working on the assumption that every babe may be a potential redeemer, he and his secretary plan to build an ideal residential educational institution in the setting of mountains and fern-gullies, and to take into it a number of carefully selected infants between the ages of two and four.

Brought up out of contact with the corroding spirit of materialistic civilisation, and given the right ethical and religious outlook, they believe that some of these girls and boys may save the world. The children are taught that "the divine purposes of man's creation can be fulfilled only by a life of loving and unselfish service". As the scheme grows and unfolds, Peter Gaunt's health becomes more and more precarious for he is in the grip of advancing tuberculosis.

Those who had the privilege of close acquaintance with Ambrose Pratt in his last years will recognise that many of the views which Gaunt expresses, many of his interests and personality traits, were closely akin to the author's own. From this viewpoint, a particularly interesting analysis of Peter Gaunt's character is made in a conversation between two characters, Mr Levison and Professor Sainton. The Professor asks his friend, "What is it that distinguishes him from the mob as far as you are concerned?" The broker replies, "I think it's the feeling that he gives you when he looks at you, that he doesn't want anything you have, but would just as soon push your barrow for you as not." Sainton comments, "The best definition of a kind spirit I've ever heard." Both agree that Peter has kindness, trustworthiness and self-control, and that he is a genuine philanthropist with a yearning to serve mankind. The professor continues, "He likes the shadows, shrinks from publicity, seems to want nothing for himself. He knows his world, has a well-informed mind . . . He thinks any old economic system would do if men's hearts were in the right place. I thought that an affectation for a bit, but I was wrong." They go on to discuss whether Peter is really a big man or not. "Maybe he's neither giant, nor middle-size, nor dwarf, but just what he seems to be." "And what is that?" says the Professor. Levison replies, "A good man – a really good man."

In the closing scene of the book when Peter is dying, he gives to his secretary Clare (who is in love with him) the essence of his outlook on life. This certainly was the outlook of Ambrose Pratt.

"The vain things and the important things are often hard to separate, their roots are intertwined. But they will always fall apart if we ask our hearts this simple question, 'What can we take with us from the world when we depart, except the love we have deserved for the kindness we have shown and the love we have bestowed?' Not our money, nor our houses, Clare; for all these things we must leave behind us. So that if we have not deserved love, we shall face God naked and with empty hands . . . There is no life except that of the spirit. The body festers when the spirit flies . . . We come from God. We stay in the world a little while, and we return to God . . . Can you doubt we were sent here for a high purpose? What purpose then, if not to leave the world better than we found it?

"Listen closely, for I am seeing very clearly. No spark of intelligence can ever perish. No flicker of consciousness can ever fade. The very idlest fancies that we entertain or fabricate are indestructible: therefore it is imperative to think straightly and sweetly always. The air we breathe and the aether that surrounds the world are crowded with deathless thoughts that strive incessantly for our attention. Some are of angelic loveliness. Some are as dreadful and distorted as creatures of the ooze. But all alike are eternally and instantly available for the benefit and injury of man. The supreme duty of the spirit is to select and use and issue into currency, thoughts that are beautiful and true. It is the function of the mind to question and to doubt the spirit's judgment. That is why mind and spirit are constantly at war. Because the mind is mortal it is proud and vain and scornfully resentful of control, but it must be subjugated to the service of the spirit if progress on this planet is to be achieved . . . Do not mourn when I have gone. My life is neither beginning nor ending. I am simply passing on. You will follow, Clare – but not yet. You have work to do. You must be faithful and strong, and grief is a wasting force. Soon a large authority will be confided to your care. You will be assailed and censured in your task. Do not hurtfully retort! To have the power to punish and to withhold punishment is to imitate God, Whose chastisement is mercy, and Whose vengeance is to pardon. Teach our babies to worship and to practise mercy. Above all, teach them this: there is only one law – it is to be kind; there is only one crime – it is to be cruel.

"Don't let our children become over-righteous Clare. It is a wrecking fault. Men will not listen to those who hold themselves superior. There is nothing more offensive to inferiority than condescension. The little-minded are many, and they are always proud and sensitive. They are not contemptible, no human being is contemptible, but when they are made to feel contemptible, they hate. They can only be placated by humility. They can only be enlightened and enlarged by love. The first duty of the magnanimous is to be meek, for magnanimity alone is capable of genuine humility. Men are not better or worse than other men: they are different, that is all. The wise know this: the ignorant who do not, shun those who seem unlike them because they feel that what is different is dangerous, and they yearn to make themselves secure. Teach our babies that to bring others to their opinions they must first become their lovers. Those who are loved are unafraid of those who love them, however different they may be. To love is to save . . . All men are worth saving Clare, equally the greatest and the least."

Ambrose Pratt was a great lover of Australian forest country, and it is pleasing to record that in Sherbrooke Forest, some twenty-five miles east of Melbourne in the Dandenong Ranges, there is a memorial to commemorate his work to protect it. In the novel from which I have quoted something of his philosophy, I quote a few sentences which show this appreciation.

"From boyhood Peter had loved the highlands of his native country with almost passionate devotion. During his exile he had climbed many mountains in the older continents. He had often been enraptured by their grandeur, but he had found them always lacking in the subtly endearing characteristics of Australia's coastal ranges: the omnipresent underbrush with its hosts of shyly flowering shrubs; the fleecy gullies spangled with sassafras and myrtles; the scintillating glory of the wattles; the rounded graciousness of the melodiously sighing she-oaks; the velvety opulence of the callitris; the dominating splendour of the Regnans – massive giants that benevolently shelter all the lesser growths; and the peculiar faintly pungent smell of the Bush, a single scent, and unforgettably distinctive, that is nevertheless compounded of a thousand perfumes; and above all, and pervading all, the softly-tinted blue-grey atmosphere which is nearly always positively visible although pellucidly transparent, and ever seems to fold the forest in a langourous embrace."

When Ambrose Pratt returned to Australia, one of the most outstanding figures was David Syme, known throughout the land as "King David". The *Age* newspaper, published in Melbourne, was at that time his sole property, and as a Scotsman who had become a passionate Australian, he used his powerful instrument to support those causes which he believed would aid and strengthen the country of his adoption. Pratt once described him as "quite the most remarkable and admirable man I have ever met". A sensational bush-ranging story which Ambrose Pratt had written was being serialised in the *Argus* newspaper at that time, and probably as a result, its circulation had substantially increased. David Syme was not pleased, and several leading articles in the *Age* suggested that this kind of story was liable to corrupt the youth of Victoria. With considerable reluctance David Syme decided he must read the serial: he confessed later to its author that he found himself waiting with no little interest for the next instalment!

One morning Ambrose Pratt found a letter waiting for him at the Athenaeum Club in Sydney. It was from David Syme, asking him if he would be willing to visit him in Melbourne and indicated that there was a vacancy on the editorial staff of the *Age* which he would like to discuss with him. It was in this way that Ambrose Pratt joined the staff of the *Age* in December, 1905. For about twelve years he contributed many articles, both special articles and leaders in support of the policies of the paper. Two of the big political issues of that time, to which the paper made a very significant contribution, were the decision to found an Australian Navy, and the fight for adequate tariff protection. To both of these Ambrose Pratt made a big personal contribution.

In 1910 a Constitution gave to South Africa self-government, and the opening of the first parliament was attended by many distinguished visitors. Mr Andrew Fisher, at that time Prime Minister of Australia, attended the opening and Ambrose Pratt accompanied his party representing the Australian Press. As a result of the visit he wrote a book called *The Real South Africa* which gave his judgments at that time of the problems, racial, political and psychological, which were facing that country. It was published fifty years ago, and in the light of what is now taking place in South and Central Africa, a few quotations may be of interest. The son of an African chieftain who had been to a university overseas said to him:

"This country once belonged to us. Essentially it is ours still. We outnumber you six to one: but we are serfs. You give us freely none but dirty work to do. You exclude us from parliament and the public services. You deny us the suffrage. You coop us up in compounds without your cities. You walk on the footpaths: you force us to tread on the roads. You are Christian and preach in your churches that all men are equal in the sight of God who made us. Yet you exclude us from the churches, which are God's Houses, and wherein equality should reign. You spit upon our colour and repudiate our rights. I tell you sir, we are quickly becoming a nation because of what you do to us. I will tell you what we want. It is to live and work in the country that belongs to us as the social equals and political peers of the white men.

23

There are those who say that our aspiration spells war. I am not one of them, but I am no prophet."

He concluded by telling Ambrose Pratt that he was the first white man in Africa who had condescended to shake him by the hand, and warned him that he would be violently censured if the fact became known.

Half a century has gone by since the book was written, and one cannot today regard the sombre outlook which he then drew as at all exaggerated, and certainly none of the major problems which he then outlined have been solved.

There is much good descriptive writing in Pratt's book, and I cannot forbear to give one example.

"Many years ago, when roaming one day with a companion through the Mattoppos, Rhodes discovered a splendid granite tor that soared above the neighbouring crags and kopjes, that commanded a breath-taking panoramic view of hill and veld in all directions, and whose smooth, rounded weather-worn summit was topped with four great oval granite boulders, separated from each other by some little space . . . Climbing to the crest of this wonderful peak, Rhodes turned from a long unhurried contemplation of the landscape to his friend. 'I shall be buried here,' he said. His grave rests in the central space between the compass boulders. The tomb has been hollowed from the solid stone; its lowly surface is almost level with the granite surface of the mound. No headstone marks the spot, nought but a recumbent sheet of bronze, embedded athwart the rock and inscribed with these simple words 'Here lie the remains of Cecil John Rhodes'.

"This is a world of diverse views and contrary opinions. To one of my companions the sight of Rhodes' grave brought cynical reflections, and evoked from him this rather mordant comment, 'The vanity of the man!' Others of the party were almost painfully affected with the simplicity, the majesty, and the solitary aloofness of spirit which seemed to have inspired the conception of such a grave. I remembered that it had been Rhodes' custom for years before his end, whenever he was worried by the sordid little things of life, or whenever he wished to be alone to give freer scope to the workings of his imperial mind, to retire unattended to the witching and mysterious solitude of the hill where now he lies in death. On that lonely rock he planned the conquest and acquisition of a territory nearly 450,000 square miles in extent.

". . . It is, I think, the most remotely silent place I have ever visited, the most seriously thought-inspiring, the most sombre, forbidding, and

24

desolately grand. While one stands gazing at the tomb, scores of lizards, blue, grey, and green, crawl from the crevices among the rocks, and steal like brilliant phantom-streaks across the tor. They are almost fearless of intruders but they make no sound. Sometimes the distant shrilling of cicadae wounds the stillness with a faint but piercing dagger-thrust of song. But soon and always the eternal hush returns, and silence reigns supreme again. What must this place of isolated gloom be like at night, when in the tropic noontide blaze it spreads a pall of gentle horror on the sensibilities – at night when the lions that teem among these pathless hills, roam abroad in search of prey, and bend their prowling steps, perhaps across the simple moveless tomb of the maker of a nation?"

In 1918 after twelve strenuous years on the editorial staff of the *Age*, Ambrose Pratt resigned. He foresaw that the close of the First World War would bring a harvest of economic and industrial problems. Some new industries had grown up in Australia, to provide commodities which it had been impossible to import. The problem of their protection was important. In addition other developments in secondary industry were beginning in the Eastern States, and a wise fiscal policy was important. Ambrose Pratt became the first Editor of a new journal, *The Industrial Australian and Mining Standard*, which offered leadership in the field of industrial economics. It also gave the Editor the satisfaction of carrying further the work and policy of his old chief David Syme, who had been dubbed "The Father of Protection in Australia".

After the break-up of the Hughes government which had steered the Commonwealth of Australia through the years of war and peace-making, years of prosperity prevailed – until the eve of the great depression. There was growing concern, however, during these years that Australia was living beyond her means. A group of five men played a leading part in those political events which formed a new party, the United Australia Party (which afterwards became the Liberal Party). These were Mr Staniforth Rickeston, Sir John Higgins, Mr R. G. Menzies, Mr Charles Norris, and Ambrose Pratt. At the end of 1931 the Scullin government was defeated and Mr Lyons became Prime Minister.

PROTECTING AUSTRALIAN FAUNA

During the last ten years of Ambrose Pratt's life, when I got to know him intimately, he never lost his capacity to surprise me by disclosing that at some period of his life he had made a contribution to yet another field of human interest. In contrast with his concern with economics and politics, he had a keen love of Nature and was a student particularly of the forms of life indigenous to Australia.

It was in pursuance of these interests that he and his close friend Sir Colin Mackenzie took the initiative in getting a government subsidy and placing the Melbourne Zoological Gardens on a satisfactory basis. Sir Colin Mackenzie occupied the Presidential Chair until he left to take charge of the Institute of Anatomy at Canberra (now a part of the National University). Ambrose Pratt was then elected to succeed him, and the section of the zoo which contains Australian fauna, as well as a memorial arch in the grounds remain as a permanent record of his service.

His view was that a zoo should not merely be a place of entertainment but a place where serious research should be done to protect and preserve natural fauna. He was himself deeply concerned for several years about the koala. As is well known, the koala is the living prototype of the "teddy-bear", a popular toy with children all over the world. When Australia was first colonised by Europeans, millions of koalas inhabited the forests of Queensland, New South Wales, Victoria, and South Australia. Their natural food, the leaves of certain types of eucalyptus trees, was available in abundance. The spread of settlement eliminated these food trees in wide areas. Bush fires, sometimes lit deliberately by graziers, provided an easy way of getting winter grass, and helped in the work of decimation. A trade in koala pelts grew up, and at one time hunter and trapper were so active that one and a half million pelts per annum were exported to the fur markets of America from Queensland alone. This was the situation in the early twenties of the present century until legislation put an end to the butchery. In the thirties, when Ambrose Pratt took up his self-imposed task of saving the koala, the animal was extinct in South Australia, and in Victoria it was estimated that only about a thousand bears remained. The species in Queensland and New South Wales were not so hardy as the Victorian species, and a Sydney authority said he had only small hope of saving them from extinction.

The koala is a marsupial mammal of great interest. The discovery of fossil remains in the Mammoth Cave of Western Australia established that it was living there in pleistocene times – a million years ago. It was a mammal that became very highly adapted to tree-climbing, and as

26

such it probably entered a biological cul-de-sac from which no general advance was possible. The eucalypt which is its food tree preceded it into Australia probably by many millions of years. It made a southern entry into Western Australia at a time when the continent was still linked with the Antarctic land-mass. The deep-sea cleft which occupied the southern and central Australian region at this period, probably forced the koala to take a northern route across to Queensland and finally down the eastern coast as it spread over the continent. Koalas never crossed into Tasmania because of the subsidence of Bass Strait.

Research established that the mortality among Victorian bears then taking place, and supposedly due to epidemics, was due to the destruction of the koala's food trees, largely through bush fires. Through hunger, the bears were driven to eat young and unsuitable eucalyptus leaves with a high cyanide or cineol content. Ambrose Pratt sought the help of the State Premier, Mr Dunstan, and with his financial assistance a representative Fauna Conference was held in Melbourne in September, 1936. As a result of this and a similar conference in the following year in Sydney, much valuable information was pooled, amendments to legislation for the protection of wild life were agreed upon, and a good deal of Press publicity was forthcoming. In both States the Forests Commission took an active interest, and wherever suitable food trees were available some permanent reservations or sanctuaries were created to assist them to multiply. There seems no doubt that these measures have now proved very successful.

The other particular interest of Ambrose Pratt was the lyre bird (menura), a songster unique to the mountainous and densely timbered belt on the eastern and south-eastern seaboard of the Australian continent. He described an encounter he had with one which regularly paid visits to a lady who lived in a little cottage in the Dandenong ranges.

"He suddenly erected his tail fanwise, and we were hard put not to exclaim at the perfection of the lyre thus startlingly displayed, and the exquisite beauty of the twelve osprey plumes, the tips of which fell in a snowy cascade over his head.

"The bird gave two melodious trills (the authentic love-call of the menura), then he advanced with mincing steps and shivering feathers towards us, singing as he came, the queer dance music of his tribe. In the dance that followed he kept perfect time with his feet and body to the music, invariably fitting three separate steps to each two beats of the tune.

"Tiring of this exercise he posed gracefully before us, one foot a little advanced, his tail rigidly fanned, his head extended, his eyes fixed on us intently, and he forthwith began his concert. He mimicked first the chuckling of young magpies in their nest, then the warbling of the parent bird. He followed with a perfect rendering of the kookaburra's long-drawn cachinations, then of two kookaburras laughing in unison. A moment later a tribe of bell-birds seemed to be performing near us, and their lovely notes were still echoing when he gave us the lash of the whip-bird and the mellow trilling of the mountain thrush. After a little pause he mewed like a cat, then he barked and snapped like an angry dog . . . Reverting to an early number he repeated the laughter of a kookaburra – and the concert was at an end."

The bird's intelligence had helped it to hold its own, but its future was by no means certain. In this instance Pratt organised the formation of a League of Youth which created a conscience among the school children of Victoria to protect the wild life of the country against depredation. Many lectures were given throughout the State and the subject received welcome Press publicity. Finally the Victorian Teachers' Union was persuaded to support the campaign in its schools wherever possible. I think Ambrose Pratt was satisfied with the result.

IN MALAYA AND THAILAND: 1930

The tin-dredging industry in Malaya and Thailand had been pioneered by Captain Edward Miles, and Australian companies had been granted under lease certain holdings of land. These leases were conditional upon the companies equipping their property by an agreed date and employing a specified number of native personnel. A tin dredger might cost at that time £150,000 and would provide employment for two or three hundred men. When the depression hit Australia, many companies holding leasehold rights found themselves unable to fulfil their covenants since capital was not available. Ambrose Pratt was asked to visit these two countries acting as a plenipotentiary on behalf of Australian interests, requesting that the companies might be permitted to continue holding these rights while deferring equipment of their properties.

When he arrived in Malaya he found that country also suffering greatly from the depression. Many dredgers were standing unused,

28

many rubber plantations were not operating, unemployment was rife, and thousands of coolies who were out of work had taken to the hills and jungles, becoming virtually outlaws and bushrangers, so that travelling was far from safe. After conferring with the local managers of Australian tin companies and also with members of the Chinese population who were interested in tin production, he came to see that the original purpose of his visit (to protect certain leases from forfeiture) was a small matter. The big task was to save this important industry from disaster. In Malaya there were altogether about a hundred tin-dredging companies – English, French, American, and Chinese. The Chinese were, however, more concerned with opencast mines than with dredging: they were responsible for more than half the annual production of tin ore, and they employed two-thirds of the men engaged in the industry. The depression had reduced the world demand for tin to about half its former level, and the price had fallen in sympathy. A few wealthy companies now saw their opportunity to profit at the expense of the weaker ones. Some worked at full blast to secure maximum output and force down the price of tin to a point where the open-cast mines (which involved higher running costs) would have to close down, together with the smaller dredging companies. The larger companies would then buy them up cheaply. Ambrose Pratt knew that the Chinese working open-cast mines would be the first to face ruin since they would be unable to fulfil their covenants as regards labour employment, and he resolved therefore to do all in his power to aid them.

The Chief Secretary, the Hon. C. W. H. Cochrane, was a British administrator of the old school and maintained a dignified exclusiveness which was almost fantastic. He would, for example, seldom give audience to an Australian, for the term "Australian" was almost synonymous with "mine manager". Faced with this bureaucracy, a subterfuge was adopted. An influential gentleman was persuaded to meet the Chief Secretary at the Club, ostensibly for a round of golf. During the course of the golf a casual remark was dropped to the Chief Secretary. "Have you met Ambrose Pratt yet?"

"No, confound him, and I am not in any hurry to do so. These Australians are all alike."

"I think you're making a mistake, Cochrane: he's quite a different sort of chap, a writer, you know, as well as a business man. I believe he's off to Bangkok very soon."

The conversation bore fruit and the next day a messenger brought an

G

invitation to Mr Pratt to meet the Chief Secretary at his home. At the interview the Chief Secretary assumed that his visitor would probably ask him for the restitution of one of the company leases which had been forfeited, or for the suspension of the labour clauses in the covenants. His secretary was with him and said, "I have the papers relative to this company here, sir."

Mr Pratt replied, "It seems too small a thing to bother about now, there are bigger issues in the balance."

"Oh!" said the Chief Secretary. "What do you want then?"

"I thought you might be interested in a plan to save the tin and rubber industries from destruction – a fate that appears almost inevitable to most people," said Mr Pratt.

"What right have you to say that?" demanded the Chief Secretary.

"What I've said is the talk of the bazaars, and the result of my own observation. Rebellion is in the air. Banditry is prevalent and on the increase. Keep on as you are going, and it will not be long before Malaya will be very difficult for anyone to save."

The Chief Secretary adopted a lofty manner and said, "I thought I was going to have the pleasure of meeting an Australian gentleman!" After a pause he added, "So you do not want to discuss the Bidor matter at all?"

"No thank you, Mr Cochrane, I have not come to discuss trifles. I have formed my own judgment of the serious state of the country, and I think your world is in serious danger of tumbling down."

Mr Cochrane dismissed his secretary and said loftily, "Then I will listen to you, Mr Pratt. Perhaps you will draw the rabbit out of your hat. I have been in this country many years, and His Majesty's Government have reposed their trust in me. Needless to say, if you come from Australia and feel you know more about the country than I do, I shall be happy to hear your views."

Ambrose Pratt outlined for him the state of the tin industry as he saw it, the falling prices, the flooding markets, the industrial and racial jealousies which were fermenting, and the attempts which were being made by certain powerful companies to exploit the weakness of others and establish a monopoly. He urged that all the industrial interests should be brought together to see if they could reach agreement, but that if not, the governments of the countries concerned in tin production should step in and enact legislation to restrict production throughout the world. He finished by asserting that Malaya could perform an immense service by taking the initiative as the world's leading tin producer and showing others what they should do.

The Chief Secretary became increasingly interested and friendly and finally asked Ambrose if he would repeat what he had said to his three technical advisers who were called in. The whole interview took between two and three hours with an interval for tiffin at which he was a guest at Mr Cochrane's family table. The upshot was that Sir Cecil Clementi the Governor-General came up from Singapore and the plan, with some minor changes was approved and sent on to the British Government with his recommendation. There is no need here to go into details of the moves which were made to attempt to defeat this proposal. Suffice to say that it was accepted by the British Government who created in London a Tin Restriction Authority. This subsequently drew into its ambit industrial and political interests of South America, Africa, America, France and Thailand, and led to a world-wide adoption of the plan. It was a remarkable personal achievement, and similar Rubber Restriction legislation followed.

Cochrane afterwards confessed to Ambrose Pratt that an aspect of the scheme which appealed to him was that it provided employment at reasonable wages in permanency for the large coolie population then engaged in the rubber and tin industries. Formerly they had been imported and used when industry was going well, and deported with inadequate charitable relief when things were not going well.

When Ambrose Pratt returned to Australia, to his surprise and profound disappointment, his colleagues and fellow directors condemned his work root and branch. It irked them that the supreme control of the industry was now out of their hands, and Pratt was made to feel that he had been a destroyer of the industry instead of its saviour. He was very tempted to resign from all association with the industry, and told me he would have done so but for the outstanding support accorded to him by one far-seeing man. Ambrose said to me:

"The experience was useful, however painful, for it taught me that the brains of big business, while superbly efficient in their special sphere, very often lack vision elsewhere, and are strangely circum-scribed in their outlook. While my friends condemned me, they were being saved. As the years passed by, it gradually became clear to them also, that the system of tin restriction had many advantages, and the control arrangements for which I was responsible, were likely to be permanent. Those who had formerly reviled me began to think it might be a good thing. It eliminated, of course, the big tin speculators, and maintained the price of this metal remarkably steady at about £210 per ton until the advent of the Second World War. Few influences are more devastating and unethical than the ability of big speculators to lower or raise prices overnight. I regard the whole scheme as an almost perfect example of the scientific adjustment of producer's capacity and consumer's needs.

"With all successful achievements there are men who rise up to claim authorship. You will appreciate that I felt some amusement when club gossip of this sort came back to me, as it often did – 'You know, we in Australia worked out the whole of the Tin Restrictions arrangements. It was an Australian plan even from its inception, and we sent Ambrose Pratt over to lay it before the government.' "

Describing his visit to Thailand in 1930, Ambrose told me that he had been in that country years before, but was then without any friends of consequence. I tell this story as he told it to me.

"I was now visiting Thailand in the interests of certain Australian companies, who, owing to the depression, had been unable to fulfil the covenants on which they held certain land. The government thus became entitled to foreclose on the leases, resume the land, and sell it back to its earlier owners, some of whom were wealthy Towkays living in Puket and some in the Federated Malay States. These were anxious to get possession of the land, intending to keep it until the depression ended and then sell at a high price. They were interested therefore in the failure of my mission. They were of course supremely courteous to me, and I to them. One of them, indeed, graciously supplied me for my journey with a 'boy', a very competent body-servant. He was about thirty-five years of age, could speak several languages, was a good writer, and could act not only as a valet but as my secretary too. It was a delightful compliment and very charmingly done, and I expressed to the Towkay who arranged it my most profound gratitude. I suspected that the boy was a spy, and that he had been so graciously provided for me that he might communicate my movements to his masters. My first task therefore, was to break him down and secure his loyalty to myself. Before leaving for Thailand, I took him up the mountains with me and treated him with a friendship and consideration not usual between master and servant. Fortune favoured me, for within a day or two he was laid up in bed in great agony with an abscess on his jaw. I took him down in my car to Kuala

Lumpur and arranged for medical and dental attention which relieved the pain and made him tremendously grateful. We then went on to Bangkok, and the whole of the first week I spent in sight-seeing and in meeting no one of importance (at any rate, to his knowledge), for I knew I could not do anything until he confessed his position and his loyalty to me. The Towkays had many influential friends in Bangkok, and if my movements had been reported to them by the boy, they would all have been countered. My consideration and friendliness finally broke him down and he confessed. He felt he had lost face, but I reassured him. I said, 'You have done well, according to your code, but it can never be wrong or involve any loss of face to leave a dishonourable course for an honourable one.' He was persuaded of this, and became thereafter my faithful servant. The letters which he wrote to his Chinese masters were written at my dictation, and needless to say, I was careful to report through him many meetings with innocuous people. It was now time to move quickly, for I knew I should have to be back in Malaya for the tin conference there.

"On Thursday about noon, I therefore dressed as a Thai, and carrying my European clothes in a small case, I made my way to the Ministry of Mines. In the middle of the day it is the custom for everyone to retire to rest for an hour or two. I expected the guards to be somnolent, and was not disappointed. Indeed, they were nearly asleep, and as it turned out, I need not have 'dressed up' at all. When I got past the guard into the building, I went into the first convenient room where there were many people asleep, and changed back into my European clothes. I found the private room of the Minister for Mines by the simple expedient of avoiding crowded apartments and seeking those that were almost empty. At length I came to a room with one occupant only. When I entered, the Minister was asleep on the sofa with a light silk robe thrown over him. It was therefore necessary to bang the door. He sat up and looked rather alarmed. Perhaps at first he wondered if I was an assassin. I 'kowtowed' to him profoundly and said, 'I am Ambrose Pratt. I hate to awaken Your Excellency, but you will remember my appointment was at one o'clock, and I have shortly to leave your estimable country for Malaya.'

" 'Ah!' he said. 'What do you want?' I replied, 'I have come on behalf of the Australian Tin Companies in your country to beg you to remember your obligation to us as pioneers in this work. I read out to him a carefully prepared statement dealing with royalties, employment figures, and the many benefits which the industry had brought to

Thailand. I pointed out that we had rendered their country a service, and that the industry had not been to the benefit of one side only. Now we had fallen on hard times, and some of our companies could no longer fulfil the covenants under which they held the leases, and it was thought by my fellow countrymen that the kind and cultured people of Thailand would show us sympathetic consideration in this difficult situation, by foregoing the lease-rents and the labour covenants while the depression lasted. I said that I hoped and prayed that His Majesty the King would relieve us of these onerous burdens. We could not keep our part of the bargain and desired their magnanimity. We recognised that Thailand could quite legally use this opportunity to take the land back which had been leased, to confiscate it, and equip it for themselves, but I pointed out that this would be contrary to the Law of Siddartha who prescribed a very different attitude to those who were in need. His Excellency listened to me in silence until my case was stated, and then in perfect English put to me a viewpoint which I recognised from the standpoint of law and business was unanswerable. My own position could only be stated from the standpoint of one seeking sympathetic consideration in time of economic disorder. Our conversation was prolonged by the Minister who spoke on many topics and expressed his appreciation of the part Australian enterprise had played in industrial development. Tea and cigarettes were brought in by servants before I left, and he had promised to convey my representations to the Council of Ministers."

Ambrose Pratt was required next day to attend a meeting of the Council of Ministers at which the King presided, and there he re-stated his case. He was later informed that the concessions he asked for would be granted to the Australian companies. Pratt at once asked for another interview with the Minister and told him that he could not accept any concession for his Australian companies unless it was also granted to the British ones. The Minister seemed surprised, but arranged for him another interview with the Council, and then Pratt explained to the Thai princes the complete identity (as it then was) of Australian and British citizenship, and how impossible it would be for an Australian to profit from an action that slighted Britain. The princes were enormously impressed by this point of view, and within a few hours Pratt was presented with a document granting the concessions equally to the British and Australian companies.

It cannot be doubted that Ambrose Pratt rendered a very great service to the tin industry. Perhaps no one else could have done what he personally was able to do. He had the great personal satisfaction of helping the Chinese in Malaya, and he made many friendships in Thailand with a people whom he came greatly to love and admire – more, I think than any others.

IN MALAYA AND THAILAND: 1939

In June, 1939 Ambrose Pratt sailed again on a visit to Malaya and Thailand, in the interests of Australian tin companies. His somewhat precarious health made him reluctant to go, but there appeared to be no one else with his experience available. His retirement from journalistic work some years earlier had been determined by active tuberculosis, and although prolonged rest and careful nursing had checked it, he easily became breathless with a little exertion, and his reserves of strength were not great.

War clouds were gathering ominously over Europe. How soon the storm would break and whether the Pacific area would be involved were questions foremost in the minds of all thoughtful men. Under the shadow of the unknown, nations like individuals, tend to draw together for security. The Prime Minister (Mr R. G. Menzies) hearing of Mr Pratt's visit asked him to undertake a commission: to explore the possibilities of closer relationships in the countries he visited.

I shall pass over business and social contacts and refer to events of international importance in which Ambrose Pratt became involved. The historian who surveys events from a sufficient distance to discern clearly their importance in the pattern of time, sacrifices through this detachment a perception of the frail personal threads of destiny on which, for a time, the whole fabric is supported. The coincidence of events in space and time with the man who has the insight and ability to shape them is always a fascinating story. Such a coincidence occurred in Bangkok on August 12th, 1939.

A glance at the map of South-East Asia makes clear the strategic importance of Thailand. From Britain's point of view, a friendly Thailand would secure from land attack, Burma on the west, and the wealthy area of Malaya on the south with the Singapore base at the extreme tip of the peninsula. Such considerations were present, not only in Ambrose Pratt's mind as he went on his mission, but they had long been present in the minds of Japanese militarists and politicians who were planning a southward advance. From the beginning of the century they had been at work preparing for this by every means at

35

their disposal: business and commercial infiltration, espionage, and all the arts of political and diplomatic usage. These efforts had not been without effect, as is clear from the rapidity with which one conquest followed another in December, 1941 and early 1942. Nippon had successfully conveyed to the minds of some of the Asiatic peoples a conception of her own strength and her future destiny. In Thailand, for example, there was a small group represented by certain Ministers in the Cabinet who believed that their country's interests would best be served by making an alliance with the rising power of Japan. Japan's propaganda had been astute and adaptable. Ambrose Pratt had foreseen Japanese intentions as early as 1906 when he had translations made of certain Japanese textbooks, but there had been the same blindness in regard to this among Australian statesmen as there had been to Hitler's menace among most statesmen in Britain.

It was then, with no illusions, but with a clear sense of the importance of a friendly Thailand, that Ambrose Pratt arrived in Bangkok. At this time two Japanese envoys were there, having brought with them documents for Thailand's approval and signature. The terms of these were believed to be substantially those of an alliance which would permit the entry of Japanese troops into Thailand under certain circumstances. Sir Josiah Crosby, the British ambassador, was desperate, and freely confessed this to Ambrose Pratt. He had been told by the Prime Minister of Thailand that any further representations of Britain's viewpoint would be unacceptable to him, and when Pratt arrived he was not even certain whether the Japanese documents had been signed or not. Crosby was an able man, a classical scholar, with a good knowledge of the Thai language in which he had written several books, and he was an experienced diplomat. He was now despondent; he felt that he had played his last cards and lost, and he was sorting out his papers in preparation for their destruction at what he believed was not a far-distant date. He felt that the scales had tipped against him, and his greeting to Ambrose Pratt was tempered with surprise and almost reproach that he should have arrived in Bangkok with two friends at such a time.

It chanced that Pratt saw in the ambassador's office a photograph of a distinguished-looking Thai officer whom he seemed to recall as a past acquaintance, and he asked who he was. Crosby replied, "That is His Excellency Luang Pibul Songgram, the Prime Minister. Why? Do you know him?" Pratt said that he might well have met him on an earlier visit to Thailand. "Pratt," said Crosby, "don't think I'm rude, but I feel like a drowning man clutching at a straw. I've failed. It's possible you might be able to do something. It may be too late. At any rate you could leave your card with him at once and try to secure an interview." Ambrose Pratt called on the Minister for Foreign Affairs with whom he was acquainted, and an interview with the Prime Minister was arranged. On August 12th a car arrived at 9.30 a.m. from the Prime Minister's department to convey Ambrose Pratt to an audience with His Excellency at the Suan Kularb Palace. His reception accorded with every formality and compliment which might be paid to a distinguished foreign visitor. As the car drove over the moat surrounding the palace, troops were drawn up, and he was escorted by officers up carpeted steps to the audience chamber. The Prime Minister was dressed in the full-dress uniform of a major-general and many of the members of his Cabinet were also present. He was introduced by Prince Varavarn, an elder statesman and general adviser to the government, who also acted as interpreter throughout the formal reception. Conversation roamed over many subjects but the occasion was not appropriate for broaching matters of which Ambrose Pratt would most have liked to speak. Feeling that he had remained long enough, he finally rose to go, whereupon the Prime Minister said, "You have risen Mr Pratt, which means perhaps that you have another engagement? I hope it is not so, as I should like you to remain a little longer for a more intimate conversation with me." Upon being assured of Mr Pratt's willingness to remain, all those present proceeded to say farewell, and retired. An informal conversation then took place. The Prime Minister spoke French fluently and understood a little English; Ambrose Pratt spoke French imperfectly, but understood it. They were able therefore to converse without an interpreter, and did so for about an hour and a half.

Luang Pibul Songgram revealed himself as a singularly noble-minded man, and a patriot with but one aim and purpose – the welfare and security of his country. He felt very heavily the burden pressing upon him of deciding what attitude his country should adopt in the coming struggle. He said frankly that Great Britain had made representations to him, and so also had Japan, for relations which might not permit of neutrality in the coming war. He had a remarkably penetrating judgment, and thought that Great Britain and France would be unable to bring Germany to book. He was singularly well-informed: he knew of the potential resources of Britain, but he knew also of her unpreparedness. He knew the weakness of France and said that once a master of strategy, she now had the "fortress" mind. He therefore considered France would fall. He thought Great Britain would fight well but would have a most difficult task. He did not think the United States of America would come into the war unless Japan struck. If, however, Japan struck at Britain in the Far East, the U.S.A. might enter, for its own ends. He asked about Australia's war effort, and Ambrose Pratt expressed the view that whereas in the previous war Australia had provided an army of some 400,000 men, now with her larger population, she might put 700,000 of the world's best fighting men in the field. "I know," said the Prime Minister, "I saw them in France." He thought nevertheless that this contribution would be but a drop in the bucket, and he was seriously weighing the possibility that the future security of his country might best be served by an understanding with the Axis powers. He made a survey of the whole field and the various possibilities, and then said, "Mr Pratt, my friends told me that you were a man of knowledge and wisdom, and now that I look into your eyes I see nothing in them but sincerity and truth. I should value your opinion as to the path of wisdom for my country."

Mr Pratt then gave his own view of the eventual outcome of the world struggle, which he believed would be long and world-wide, and he concluded by saying, "Your Excellency, may I venture to ask you a personal question? Are you a Buddhist?"

"Yes, certainly, Mr Pratt."

"Then a much greater one than I has given you the perfect advice for all such situations, when he said, 'Follow the Middle Path.' I am sure there never was an occasion for your country when strict neutrality was more the path of wisdom."

There was a prolonged silence, and the Prime Minister finally broke it by saying: "My friend, you do not advise me to help your country! You give me disinterested advice – strict neutrality."

"By this course," said Ambrose Pratt, "it is possible you may not be protected from either side. When great nations are fighting for their lives they do not always respect the rights of others. But I am quite sure that the Buddhist 'Middle Path' is the right one for your country."

"How mild, how just is your language," said the Prime Minister. "I shall not make up my mind now, but I shall consider carefully what you have said."

As the interview closed Ambrose Pratt made one request, "If Your Excellency should decide not to accept my advice, may I beg of you that you will allow me to visit you once more before you implement your decision?"

"Yes, Mr Pratt, I think I can promise you that."

"There is one other matter I should like to ask Your Excellency. I am going to call on Sir Josiah Crosby."

"Oh! Do you know him well?"

"No, Your Excellency, I have only met him recently here. I should like to know if you feel there would be any objection to my relating to him the broad facts of my interview with you?"

"No, Mr Pratt, I should wish you to be free to use your own judgment in the matter."

As they were saying farewell Mr Pratt mentioned the anxiety with which he would await His Excellency's decision, and the Prime Minister replied that he also would feel deep concern until the matter was settled. When Sir Josiah Crosby received an account of what had passed, he started to hope again. He asked Ambrose Pratt if he would write a report of his interview for immediate despatch to Lord Halifax, at that time British Foreign Secretary. "Tell him," said Crosby, "the fix we're in out here, and how much it would mean to us to have a fleet at Singapore." Pratt complied with Crosby's request and this letter was sent.

Four days later, on August 16th, a dinner was given by Luang Pibul Songgram at the Sauraromya Palace. Some forty persons were present comprising Ministers of the government, diplomats and their wives. Guests were being received in an ante-room by the Deputy-Minister for Foreign Affairs. Pratt and Crosby who arrived there early, stood in a position where they could watch the guests arrive. Crosby said, "We shall soon know whether your advice has been accepted by the Prime Minister. If the Japanese and German ambassadors are not here, it will mean that he is following the course you suggested. That will be his delicate way of letting you know."

As they watched and waited these two diplomats failed to arrive and the guests were conducted into the banqueting hall. As they sat down to dinner a Thai lady whispered to Mr Pratt, "You must not recognise any of the waiters here tonight. On such occasions as this they are all high officials in State departments." After dinner and speeches an atmosphere of pleasant informality developed and some of the younger persons gathered round Ambrose Pratt to cross-question him and listen to his conversation. Ambrose had a considerable knowledge of Buddhism and its history and this quickly became recognised. The cultured Thai is a deeply religious man and as the evening wore on many of them questioned him about the basis of their faith and the nature of ultimate things. He made many close friends among them, and long after his visit some continued to write to him about spiritual matters.

The remaining days passed rapidly. Unfortunately Ambrose Pratt was not well enough to accept the Prime Minister's invitation to visit Lop Buri, the Aldershot of Thailand. He particularly regretted this for it was a signal honour, not previously extended to any European, and it was conveyed to mark the Prime Minister's confidence in Pratt's integrity. At the request of the Prime Minister Pratt paid him a farewell visit, and discovered that he was suffering from a feverish illness with a nurse moving in and out of the apartment. The Prime Minister repeated the friendly assurances which he had previously given and asked Mr Pratt to convey to the Australian Prime Minister his desire that the two countries should exchange Ministers at an early date. He presented Ambrose Pratt with an autographed portrait of himself.

The friendship which was formed between Luang Pibul Songgram and Mr Ambrose Pratt was continued in correspondence during the early years of the war. Ambrose showed me a letter from His Excellency dated May 18th, 1941 in which he said:

"I do not think I need add anything else, except an assurance that Thailand's policy still remains one of strict and impartial neutrality and of equal friendship with all the powers. You will therefore observe that Thailand has not deviated from the Buddhist 'Middle Path'."

Events afterwards moved too quickly for reciprocal diplomatic representation to be effected at that time. On Monday December 8th, 1941 Mr Churchill informed the British House of Commons that he had the previous day sent a message to the Prime Minister of Thailand as follows:

"There is a possibility of imminent Japanese invasion of your country. If you are attacked, defend yourself. The preservation of full independence and sovereignty of Thailand is a British interest, and we shall regard an attack on you as an attack on ourselves."

It is now a matter of history that a Japanese invasion fleet sailed up the Gulf of Siam and landed her troops on the comparatively undefended southern coast. Thailand and other countries were engulfed on Japan's southward march.

Before these tragic events closed the door two other matters eventuated. It was natural that when seeking a Consul-General in Australia, the Thai Government should invite Ambrose Pratt to represent them in this capacity. After consultation with the Prime Minister of Australia he agreed to do this. Shortly afterwards (on October 5th, 1941) Pratt received a cable informing him of the bestowal of the Order of the White Elephant, one of the highest Orders which can be conferred on foreign persons, and one but rarely given.

CONVERSATIONALIST

Ambrose Pratt was one of the most fascinating conversationalists to whom I have ever listened. During the closing years of his life my wife and I were frequent visitors at his home and we heard him discourse on many things. Sometimes it would be stirring drama on which by some fortunate (or unfortunate) chance, his own life had impinged. He could tell a tale brilliantly, but one knew that however desperate or tense the situation, at the right moment Ambrose would wave the wand of his superb gifts, and the tangle would be resolved. Sometimes he would provide brilliant analyses of Australian contemporaries, and at other times he would talk about the fascinating and complex structure of the human self; especially of those deeper regions of mind in which he had been himself an explorer.

I think probably few men in Australia in the early years of the century can have enjoyed a wider circle of acquaintance than he did. I listened to many brilliant character analyses of some of these men: of statesmen such as Edmund Barton, Alfred Deakin, William Morris Hughes and Robert Gordon Menzies; of industrialists such as H. V. Mackay, Sydney Myer, Achalen Palfreyman, and others. I shall illustrate this by recording here what he once told me about his close friend Sir Colin Mackenzie:

"Sir Colin Mackenzie was one of my closest friends up to the time of his death on June 29th, 1938. He had a broad forehead, a splendid long-headed skull, and intensely blue-violet eyes from the outer sides of which radiated a few happy furrows which counterbalanced the firmness of his mouth and chin. He died at the early age of sixty-one, an outstanding orthopaedic surgeon and brilliant comparative anatomist, whose work was known all over the world. At the age of twenty-one he graduated in medicine from the University of Melbourne, subsequently he was a resident medical officer there. After this he was for two years at the Children's Hospital during which time he came in contact with the tragic results of infantile paralysis. It was the experience which led to his dominant interest: that of eliminating the results of this scourge by proper muscle treatment and re-education. When twenty-six he first visited Europe, took his F.R.C.S. at Edinburgh and worked at Heidelberg in Germany with the eminent orthopaedist Professor Vulpius, and also with Sir Robert Jones in Liverpool. On this foundation he built his own ideas of muscle re-education and treatment.

"His other great interest was the comparative anatomy of Australian fauna. He had a laboratory in St Kilda Road and carried out hundreds of dissections to elucidate problems of structure and function. It was fascinating to watch how these different currents of interest flowed together in his mind: the scientific interest of the comparative anatomist was constantly stimulating with some new idea the compassionate nature of the orthopaedic surgeon. It was his close study of the well-developed deltoid region of the koala, and his observation of the koala's movement of its upper limbs in its native habitat, out of which came his upper arm abduction splint in 1908.

"As his work on infantile paralysis developed, he left general practice and became a consultant in Collins Street. His great reputation helped him to become financially independent, so that he was able to give the greater part of his time to a free surgical clinic which he opened in Melbourne, and to his anatomical researches.

"In 1915, soon after the outbreak of the First World War, he went to England and there collaborated with Sir Arthur Keith in making collections of war-injuries. Several valuable and comprehensive anatomical collections were made. For one of these an American University offered £50,000 – an offer which was declined. Later in the war, he was in charge of a muscle re-education department at a large military hospital at Shepherds Bush, London. Many thousands of war-injured soldiers passed through his hands and had the benefit of his skill. In 1918 he returned to Australia and continued his researches. His anatomical museum became as enormous in its size as it was valuable and indeed unique in its character. It was offered to the nation, and in 1924 was accepted by an Act of Parliament in which a National Museum of Australian Zoology was founded. In 1930 this was converted into the Australian Institute of Anatomy, and his valuable collection was housed at Canberra – he being appointed the first

Director of the Institute. He believed that this would become a national asset much as the Hunterian Museum of the Royal College of Surgeons was in London.

"He was a shy, retiring and almost bashful man, but when in 1929 he received the honour of knighthood for his services, this recognition greatly pleased him.

"He seldom wrote letters, but he used to keep in touch with me about his discoveries by visiting. I remember well one day in 1931 which was extremely wet. There came a ring at the door, and on going to answer it, there stood Colin with a large box under his arm. He had driven down from Canberra, and was obviously preoccupied with some matter of importance. He had scarcely got inside before he said, 'I want to have a talk with you, Ambrose. Have you got a good light?' He proceeded to open the box and brought out of it a plaster cast of a head. 'That's a model of Hitler's head,' he said. He had had it sent out to him by one of his old professors in Germany. Then he produced a sheaf of papers and showed me the standard measurements of all the famous long-headed skulls known to him.

"He said, 'I don't think you understand how important this is, Ambrose. The bulk of the German people are a square-headed race, marked by docility and executive ability. They can be dominated and led. Give them a job to do, and it will be done with painstaking thoroughness and ability. But here is a pronounced long-headed skull, with constructive imagination – and he is coming into leadership of this people.'

"He was very moved – almost upset by his discovery – and he went on, 'Ambrose, this is the worst thing that has happened for a very long time. It is full of danger and menace for mankind.' He was full of gloomy forebodings, as though he sensed that disaster for Europe inevitably lay ahead, in this strange conjunction of circumstances.

"He had one of the finest brains of any man I have met. He was a man of the noblest ideals and the most generous spirit. He was indeed a perfect example of the materialist scientist united to humanitarianism at its best. We occasionally talked about ultimate things, but here we were poles apart. He believed that when anything died, it just passed out for ever. My own perceptions were incredible to him, and they struck no answering chord. My friendship and regard for him were such that I longed to compel him to see that which lies behind the material world: but I was forbidden. All men must discover truth for themselves."

Ambrose Pratt undoubtedly possessed a brilliant mind, particularly well developed on the side of creative imagination and memory. He could produce information of the most diverse kind, from the history of early Asiatic kingdoms to the habits of rare insects. There were few topics of conversation to which he could not contribute some interesting and relevant comment, frequently with personal experience. Acquaintances listening to some of his stories and anecdotes frequently entertained a good deal of scepticism as to their fact-content. This was inevitable, for he indulged his instinct for the dramatic and picturesque, and he used hyperbole more than most. His close friends appreciated this use of bright colours and allowed for it, but were well aware that he had often been involved in strange and sometimes historic events which he had assisted in shaping. His purely intellectual judgments were, I think, as much likely to be at fault as most men's, but his intuition was of an unusual order. In general discussion he tended to take the view which was opposite to the prevailing one and defend it with the eloquence and intransigence of a good lawyer. He had the self-confidence and persuasiveness of an advocate who never admits he is defending a weak case, and I think he got a quiet amusement out of this. But if his defence was ever beginning to appear weak then he had a most disconcerting knack of lifting the whole subject on to a high moral plane where to do other than agree would be almost reprehensible! Then one could almost catch the twinkle of amusement in his eye.

Ambrose Pratt lived very modestly in a little house in Surrey Hills, Melbourne. He once said to me, "I never in my life cared for making money or for money. Whenever I worked at any job where monetary rewards accrued, what instigated me was either the pleasure I derived from the work itself or the consciousness of an opportunity to do some good. I have never been what men call rich, nor have I ever wanted for the simple things I have required." For a man whose interests were so deeply and widely involved in human affairs, he kept his spirit singularly detached from these things. Two qualities shone in Ambrose Pratt more clearly than any others: kindness and benevolence. It was one of his cardinal principles to do all the good he could as quietly and unobtrusively as possible: in this way, he believed the spirit of man grew in stature. I have always believed that one of the final tests of true greatness rests in a genuine humility. If a man, seeing a task that needs doing, is prepared to do it and let others have praise for the achievement; if a man's satisfaction is that the good thing shall be done, with no desire for recognition, and with indifference to whom credit is given, he has one of the qualities which mark greatness. Ambrose Pratt was well on the way.

During the last twelve months of his life he had no reserves of strength, and breathlessness followed hard upon any undue exertion. He told a few friends he would not be staying very long and his visits to the city became fewer. The last three weeks of his life he was confined to bed with increasing weakness and respiratory difficulty. He passed into a coma in the early hours of Thursday, April 13th, 1944 and breathed his last about one o'clock that afternoon.

THE KINGDOMS OF THE MIND

Of those who knew Ambrose Pratt as a vivid and colourful personality, well-informed, and entering into public life at many points, very few if any, realised that he lived an inner and private life where his deepest interests lay. He was at heart a mystic and an explorer in fields of knowledge where but few Westerners find their way. It was as a consequence of this inner life, and certain convictions he had formed, that he entered so fully into everyday affairs, believing that his mysticism required that he should seek every opportunity of serving his fellow men. "The balanced life", he said, "revolves around twin foci: one is that of solitary meditation and the gathering of self-knowledge, the other is that of service to others. Both contribute to spiritual progress and development."

I wrote to him on one occasion of the pleasure I had received from reading Younghusband's book *The Challenge of Everest*. In his reply he said:

"On those heights have been fabricated the surest methods of approach to a study of the problems of life that anywhere exist, and there too, has been made the rather terrible discovery that the real Himalayas exist only in the mind – vast ranges, high peaks, and bottomless declivities which most of us shrink from exploring, being more than content to apply our faculties exclusively to the business of climbing concrete Kanchenjungas, when not for the moment engaged in the enthralling pastime of battling with our brothers for a strip of desert or a loaf of bread."

Having related something of the outer life of Ambrose Pratt I shall now attempt the more difficult task of presenting a few aspects of his inner journeyings. He told me that as a young man he had possessed a consciousness of undeveloped powers within himself and an equally compelling urge to find a way of realising them. In

H

this he met with a measure of success, and he was in later years interested to find that his own methods differed but little from those which have been known from time immemorial by the yogis of India.

In the course of his exploration he discovered how to pass through a series of stages which culminated in freedom of his consciousness from the physical body. (I did not at that time know of the phenomenon of astral projection or out-of-the-body experience.) He spoke of this process as a "going-out", and said that when he "went out" he found himself in the company of others on the same level of development – benign and benevolent persons, who offered their friendship and help and looked for it in return. He said it was not accurate to talk of seeing, hearing and feeling on that level, but rather of possessing one great faculty of apprehension in which these senses seemed to be merged into one. Compared with earthly existence this state was infinitely more pleasant and desirable and, naturally enough, he had often not desired to return. These benevolent spirits were, however, insistent on the importance of returning and helped him to do so. The body, in the absence of the spirit which energises it was like a battery slowly running down, or a flywheel with the power cut off: the life ebbs very slowly away. He said that the reanimation of the body could be somewhat painful, especially if the dislocation had been rather prolonged. He was satisfied that John Henry Newman must have had some similar experience to his own, for he regarded the description in the *Dream of Gerontius* as perfectly describing an experience which he had gone through in his early experiments.

> *I can no more; for now it comes again,*
> *That sense of ruin which is worse than pain,*
> *That masterful negation and collapse*
> *Of all that makes me man; as though I bent*
> *Over the dizzy brink of some sheer infinite descent;*
> *Or worse, as though*
> *Down, down for ever I was falling through*
> *The solid framework of created things,*
> *And needs must sink and sink*
> *Into the vast abyss.*

With practice he acquired considerable facility in making this transition, and he told me that from the normal sleep-state, this transition took place very frequently with him – and quite involuntarily. He stressed many times how difficult it was to retain in the form of

46

memory much of the experience, which seemed most vivid and clear when he was actually in it. It apparently faded with considerable rapidity after regaining normal consciousness, just as most dreams do. He was satisfied that the human brain structure was not yet evolved to a point where it could be anything but a very imperfect vehicle of the spirit's experience. The fragments which he was able to retain, he carefully recorded in journals to which he gave me access. How far these records were elaborated on the ordinary conscious level it is impossible to say: I do not think he would have been sure himself. He told me that in earlier years when in an adventurous mood, he had endeavoured to go as far as possible into the "beyond" and that on one occasion some friendly voice speaking with great authority told him that if he persisted in this he would inevitably neglect the tasks for which he had been incarnated, and would have to pay the price of coming back again to fulfil them. From then onwards, apart from the involuntary excursions in sleep, he did not "go out" unless for some good purpose in which he felt justified. My desire to learn as much of his viewpoint as possible led me to return to this and related themes again and again. I shall present something of this in dialogue.

Self: What do you understand happens when you enter a state of trance, and leave your body?
Ambrose: The psycho-physical consciousness retires from its customary physical habitat and merges with pure consciousness. The pure consciousness has its own store of knowledge otherwise acquired, it has vast powers of communication with, and comprehension of members of the spirit universe who occupy a plane similar to that of the person experimenting. It was always my dream and wish to bring back with me on my return, definite recollections of what I had learned and the people I had met during my excursion. I invariably found that the ineptitude of my physical machine stood in the way of impressing anything like a complete memory of what had happened on my psycho-physical consciousness.
Self: What are the dominant feelings you have when "out"?
Ambrose: The spirit is clearly in a world of more dimensions than this one, and there is an impression that the spirit is restored to unity and simplicity. It is the terrestrial experience which then seems tangled and complex. All the spiritual faculties corresponding to the physical senses of seeing, hearing, touching, etc., are merged in one great faculty of apprehension. One of the dominant feelings is that of

security. In earthly life, everything is uncertain and insecure: there, one is wrapped in security. There is also an enormous sense of liberation and freedom from the limitations of the body. There is an increased sense of both knowledge and power, and a vast capacity to cultivate those things which you feel should be cultivated. Thus, each prepares himself here to exercise the things he feels most worth while there. We realise the experience we have built ourselves up to receive. Above all, there is a completely pervading atmosphere of friendliness and goodwill.

Self: Has Time any significance in that world?

Ambrose: I should say that I felt timelessness as one of its characteristics.

Self: But does not what you describe as a sequence of spiritual experiences imply a time-sequence?

Ambrose: This may not necessarily be the case, for your interpretation in this way is presumably based upon your experience in the body.

Self: Is there any sense of a Supreme Spirit: any increased awareness of God?

Ambrose: There is definitely an enlarged awareness of Divinity: one might almost say that it is realised for the first time. But all the familiar conceptions of the ordinary religious person who talks as though he could be on intimate terms with God are self-deluding blasphemies. When I penetrated the farthest there was still a realisation of the remoteness of God, as of One infinitely far beyond the human spirit – an approach nearer to Whom could only come through self-discipline and improvement through aeons of time. I use the term "time" to convey the sense of almost endless effort. The inner awareness of Divinity is certainly increased however.

Self: Where does Jesus Christ come in?

Ambrose: I never found Him, nor had any of the other spirits I knew. But I absorbed as it were, a realisation that He *is*, and that there are others like Him. There is no one channel of salvation; all salvation is the development of the power within us. Each of us achieves advancement by doing sincerely what *he* sees should be done. Hence arises the great law of tolerance and compassion. After this experience there is no room for contempt of others, remembering that in such a way a higher spirit might look upon one's self. I once put the question, to whom, I don't know, – "Where is God."? The answer came back gently chiding, and suggesting something of amusement, "To what loneliness you condemn your Deity." I brought back this impression: there is no yardstick to measure the Infinite.

48

Self: What is Thought?

Ambrose: Thinking is one of the creative functions of spirit, but *thought*, the product of this process, has a real objective existence apart from its creator. Thought is indestructible: that which is thought affects all other spirits throughout the universe. Other spirits can accept or reject the thoughts around them. Hence the great importance of right thinking. Thought may perhaps be compared with Light: once emitted from the lamp it goes on for ever. This is not speculation, it is what I know to be true.

Self: We both accept the view that knowledge of future events (precognition) is a possibility. In some sense then, there is a predetermined future. Can you reconcile this with freewill which we also accept?

Ambrose: I cannot reconcile them, but I accept them both. I think it is probable that one of them (determinism) belongs to this order, and the other (complete freewill) belongs to a higher order. Is it not possible that events which may be undetermined in a world of higher dimensions, may be determined in one of three dimensions? The spirit, *qua* spirit, has within wide limits complete freedom of choice. When, however, it is tied up with a body as in terrestrial experience, the measure of its freedom depends upon (*a*) the quality of the spirit, (*b*) the quality of the physical mechanism through which it works in the world, and (*c*) the quality and extent of the association between the two. We all know that sometimes a fine spirit can triumph over all the limitations of a poor, crippled or distorted body. On the physical side, it is the pyramidal cell layers of the prefrontal cortex which the spirit is particularly striving to develop as an aid to fuller expression in this world.

Self: Can you throw any light on reincarnation: the rebirth of spirits in life after life upon earth?

Ambrose: I know it takes place, but I am not in a position to say that it is a universal rule. It may possibly be that some spirits find a road of self-development without incarnation, while others, by choice or otherwise, are committed to terrestrial life. For the latter it is most reasonable to suppose that many terrestrial lives take place until spiritual development is such that there is no obligation to return to Earth. At this stage there is freedom to choose the future path. I know that occasionally a spirit which has attained this freedom chooses to return as a volunteer for some great task, or perhaps to satisfy some urge within itself for further service here. Sometimes by stepping down we may progress. When such a soul voluntarily reincarnates, it places itself once more under judgment as to its motives and acts, and of course temporarily relinquishes the complete freedom of choice it has won. In doing so it is, however, fortified by a strong and clear intuition, by the urge and capacity to open up the channels between the pure and the self-aware consciousness, and by a knowledge thereupon of its past.

Self: Are such enlightened spirits common? How do you recognise them?

Ambrose: No, by no means common. I suppose I may have met five or six in the course of my life. The recognition is wholly intuitive. I knew one, a close friend, who came back through love of human-kind whom he sought to inspire through music. He was an eminent musician. He realised his high purpose was not succeeding as he had hoped, and he retired from this life voluntarily – as these rare spirits all have the power to do.

Self: Have you yourself any memory of former lives on earth?

Ambrose: Yes, but only fragmentarily. The last time I remember was very long ago as we measure time.

Self: Some of the mystics use language which suggests that at the depth of our pure consciousness, we are all members one of another, as though our individuality was merely that of coral islands appearing above sea-level, but all merging on the sea-bed. Is this your impression?

Ambrose: No. Our pure consciousness is our own possession. We are independent evolving spirits, although it is a social universe.

Self (May 21st, 1940): Have you ever had any light thrown on the outcome of the present war?

Ambrose: I do not seek to know the future: what is gained by it? I was, however, assured on one occasion, (a) that no spiritual values would perish, (b) that I need have no anxiety for my spiritual kindred or myself, and (c) that I must under all circumstances keep myself free from hatred.

Self: You once said that if an all-wise coroner held an inquest on everyone who died, he would rarely need to pronounce any other verdict than suicide or accidental death. Did you mean that the powers of man's spirit to counter disease and old age are quite adequate to these tasks if we knew how to use them?

Ambrose: Yes, definitely. Some day it will be realised that without the spirit's will to live all the drugs in the world are useless. Perhaps when knowledge advances further, the fortification of the spirit of a sick person will be recognised as an important part of all treatment. The "spirit" surrounds and infuses its body, although these spatial terms quite imperfect. In the very young child less of the spirit is incorporated, as it were; as development proceeds the spirit immerses itself to an increasing degree in the body. But even the best developed body never becomes an adequate vehicle for the spirit, much of which finds through it no expression.

There is no such thing as death of the spirit. From any living creature the spirit may be driven out, and what remains when it has left is matter. In living creatures two opposing sets of forces are at work: on the one hand those of accumulation, and on the other those of dispersal and expenditure. The latter are always operative, but in infancy and adolescence the former are dominant. At maturity a balance is achieved, but after this, very slowly, the forces of acquisition which have made for youthfulness and vigour lose their power, and the process of ageing begins. The spirit carries with it into the body it creates, a host of curiosities, desires, expectations, passions and anxieties, and as the body develops it charges it with these things and it uses the charged body for the satisfaction or assuagement of its emotions. Unless the spirit has the knowledge and will to control them they augment those forces which make for dispersion.

But I can see no reason why a human life could not be prolonged indefinitely: in fact, I know it can be done. The physical condition of the body could be maintained at that stage at which the experiment was effectively undertaken. But power always involves responsibility. A person who has the knowledge and undertakes such an experiment, is accepting a very heavy responsibility – which I for my part, have no wish to accept.

Self: I suppose that even in a young child, the spirit is mature?

Ambrose: As old as time. You will appreciate that a spirit which is engaged in building a body – a task which it has done many times before – may not always be very satisfied or pleased with its creation and may at times of serious illness, when there is generally a looser attachment of spirit and body, wonder whether not to retire. This is particularly so with the finer and more advanced spirits, for whom the prospect of terrestrial life is neither so attractive, nor the urge so great. The years of babyhood and childhood must sometimes be very irksome to more advanced spirits. Yet no one abandons a worth-while task without incurring consequences. All tasks which have been undertaken for some good purpose must be completed: the spirit's progress depends on that.

Self: What do you conceive in broad terms to be the meaning or purpose of the universal process?

51

Ambrose: I believe a vast experiment is being made in which spirits are experimenting with new forms of expression, using the matter of the universe to do so. It may be that in the end it will be possible for a race of psycho-physical beings to pass freely and at will from one world-level to another. They may have such complete understanding of, and control over matter that they can construct for themselves far more refined, sensitive and adequate bodily instruments than are now available. Such instruments may be as indestructible as the psyche itself, or at least destructible only at will. I believe all the spirits participating in this vast cosmic experiment are volunteers, but having once undertaken the task, there can be no turning back.

The main instrument of this great experiment appears to be strife, as represented by the contending opposites, bestial and spiritual; good and evil; kindness and cruelty. In the absence of this tension man settles down to an enjoyment of life and the progress of the experiment is retarded. Thus it comes about that nations decay and civilisations perish, being challenged or overridden by peoples they once despised. The fittest from the point of view of the experiment survive: the least-fit perish.

Chief among the secondary purposes of terrestrial existence I put the gathering of wisdom, i.e. the education of the spirit. At its incarnation each spirit brings with it all its gathered wisdom and knowledge, which are the content of the pure consciousness and not normally accessible to the self-aware consciousness. Under these limitations every choice made is without more than a very limited knowledge of the consequences. So in the end, good is not chosen because it brings happiness, or evil avoided because it brings suffering, but good is chosen because the spirit is good. Our universe is not constructed to operate on a system of external rewards and punishments. Every right choice contributes to that spirit's progress and every wrong choice to its decline. For those who do not make a higher choice the wheel turns round once again until the same moral alternatives are presented – perhaps in a different life, perhaps in different terms. But a spirit's progress depends upon its choosing rightly.

All perfection is only relative: the achievement of one stage is the beginning of another. There is no finality, but an endless prospect and an endless way.

Using Wordsworth's words in a sense different from that which the poet intended, I used to feel after such conversations:

52

all paradise
Could, by the simple opening of a door,
Let itself in upon him.

THOUGHTS ON WAR

When the Second World War broke out, Ambrose was staying at Pahang in Malaya. I had written to him about the international situation, and from one of his letters extract the following:

"Don't suffer the war to worry you overmuch, Raynor! It had to be. I hoped it might have been postponed till next year, but I realised fully I hoped for a foolish thing, even while I was hoping most sincerely, because diseases spread and flourish when they are not strenuously and capably opposed – and the world has too long been watching idly the growth of the worst ailment mankind has yet experienced."

A fortnight later (September 27th, 1939) he wrote again.

"I find it's idle to try to put on paper what I want to say to you about the war. I can feel that both you and Mary are too troubled about it. You do not suspect it, I fancy – but I am a thorough-going pacifist and believe that the proper way to treat thieves and murderers is to give them one's goods and one's life – should they demand these trivialities. But I am not troubled at all, because it is a fact, and therefore inevitable, and therefore to be suffered and endured, and turned to laughter rather than tears. Also it is probably (but of this I am not sure) a biological necessity.

"Of this, however, I am very certain: this war will destroy nothing of permanent value to mankind and it will cleanse the spirits of many living and of millions to be born. And is it not exhilarating to feel that God is no more satisfied with us than we are, in our deep hearts, with ourselves; and no more despairing of us than we are of ourselves, but is still cannily experimenting with us, and therefore willing to improve us.

"But there's no use, Raynor, I can't set down my inmost thoughts, the ones that matter – only the surface scum of partly sweet and partly terrible reflections."

I have included these two extracts written at a time of world crisis, because they present what some would say were contradictory viewpoints. I would say rather that they present an inner tension – the tension between realism and idealism, between present wisdom and ultimate wisdom, between the course which reason prescribes as wiser and that which spiritual insight prescribes as nobler. It is the tension between the human and the divine found in most thoughtful men, a tension from which Ambrose Pratt, with his great gift of detached contemplation of the world, had not yet quite freed himself. He died before Hiroshima and therefore did not live to see mankind enter upon the nuclear age.

Ambrose passed over at the age of seventy to a world with which in some measure he was already familiar. Few men of his generation can have had a greater variety of experience or touched more sides of life with distinction. He had explored the inner worlds as far as he was permitted to go. He had travelled in many different parts of the world and done adventurous things. He had taken an active part in politics behind the scenes, he had been a journalist and editor, an economist and a successful writer of imaginative books. He possessed marked artistic gifts if he had cared to concentrate upon them, but he set them aside. He was a mystic at heart but this interest he kept secret except from a friend or two. He moved with great ease and friendliness among other men, but always there was a subtle air of distinction in his personality which others freely recognised. Partly it derived from his fine and gracious presence and from his natural courtesy, but in essence it seemed to me to reflect some quality of a deep level. He moved through ordinary life with an inward confidence in his power to meet whatever it brought to him. Yet this went with a true humility which was most clearly seen in this: that he preferred to work in the background. Yet, when something worth while had been achieved he pushed lesser men forward to receive the thanks and appreciation.

In the journal of some of his intimate thoughts I read, after his death, the following words:

"Looking back over a long life the only things I can remember of which I am not ashamed are occasional little acts of magnanimity. The only things I can remember of which I am a little proud are occasional acts of kindness done at some little cost and trouble to myself. And this is true of every man and woman in the world."

A few days before he died, when he was too ill to receive any visitors, I wrote him a little note (which I have reason to believe he read). It was to tell him that I had cherished his friendship and to convey to him my conviction that we should meet again further along the road. In one sense we have done so – as the succeeding essay will disclose – but, the best is yet to be.

The Bridge Across Death

"If this little life were all, if our brief little existence on the lighted stage were the grand reality, if there were no invisible sphere, no great communion of minds, no shared adventures of spirit, we would not have the feeling of moving through a haunted world."

S. Radhakrishnan

Our Western culture-pattern has no generally accepted philosophy of life and death. There is no prevailing recognition of profounder levels of being to which human life is related. The most characteristic activities are scientific discovery, technological progress, commercial life and pleasure-seeking. Death is little thought about except when it intrudes on our personal circle, and then the dominant thoughts are of sadness or tragedy. Christianity affirms its belief in the continuance of life after death, but its voice tends to be vague and comforting rather than precise and convincing. The majority of scientists whose studies keep them absorbed in the sensory world, easily forget – if they have ever recognised the fact – that the observing self belongs to another order of phenomena, even more worthy of study. The small minority of thoughtful people who have made a study of psychical research generally agree that certain powers of the mind, often labelled telepathy, clairvoyance, psycho-kinesis, precognition, etc., are established beyond doubt. But this, curiously enough, has made it more difficult to establish the survival by the human mind of the change we call death. Some (including myself) looking at all the variety of evidence accumulated and sifted in the last eighty years are satisfied that if survival is not in the strictest sense "proven", it can be taken as so highly probable, that for practical purposes it is the same thing. Others surveying the field come to a different conclusion.

In this essay I propose to set down evidence which came to me – which I regard as one of the most remarkable experiences of my life. I do not present this as *proving* anything to my reader: but I cannot deny that it has had a profound influence on my own judgment of the issue.

Some years ago I read with much interest two books written by Miss

Geraldine Cummins called *The Road to Immortality* and *Beyond Human Personality*. These were stated by the author to be automatic scripts and purported to have come from, or been inspired by Frederic W. H. Myers (who died in 1901). Myers' name will be familiar to most of my readers as that of an eminent classical scholar of Cambridge, a minor poet, and one of the founders of the Society for Psychical Research last century. He was an indefatigable research worker in this field, and author of the famous book *Human Personality and its Survival of Bodily Death*. Having formed a favourable judgment in regard to Miss Cummins' claim, I was desirous of meeting her, and she on her part knew of me as author of *The Imprisoned Splendour*. In October, 1953, being in London, my wife and elder daughter and I paid a social call on Miss Cummins. Before leaving I said to her, "I have never had any first-hand communication with 'the other side'. To receive some really convincing evidence would mean a great deal to me. You know, there is a big difference between belief and conviction." She was kind enough to say that sometime, she would see what she could do, and it would help if I left her some of my handwriting to be a psychic link.

At this point I shall digress to comment on the nature of automatic writing. There are some persons, usually called mediums or sensitives, who can at will withdraw conscious control from its normal level and pass into what we call a trance state. In this state, the subconscious mind may use the apparatus of speaking or writing to express itself. It may write or draw or paint with ability which that person does not normally possess. It may dramatise with consummate acting skill, and present different aspects or facets of itself as though they were separate personalities. This is of course very interesting and useful from the standpoint of psychotherapy. Furthermore, in the trance state, a medium is often able to exercise a degree of paranormal power; the mind of the medium may make contact at subconscious levels with another mind (telepathy), reproducing the material thus obtained. Such information would normally be regarded as a private memory of the other mind. We must also recognise the possibility that through an entranced medium, discarnate persons *may* in fact communicate with the living. Telepathic rapport may be quite possible between a *discarnate* mind and the subconscious mind of the medium. Sometimes the automatic writing of a medium may show a resemblance, even amounting to identity, with the handwriting of a deceased person (which the medium may not be aware of having seen before). At other times the automatic script may show little or no resemblance to that of the deceased communicator. These may correspond to two different modes of communication by a deceased person. In the first type there is a near-physical control of the medium's writing mechanism; in the second type, it is likely that ideas or thoughts are planted telepathically in the medium's subconscious mind, and the latter finds the words in which to reproduce them.

To sum up, if A. B. visits a medium and receives a script which purports to be a message from his deceased friend X. Y., and if this script shows characteristics of X. Y including memories shared between them and with no other person, then a decision has to be made whether X. Y. has been in fact communicating, or whether the medium at subconscious levels has been thought reading and has derived all his information from memories in A. B.'s subconscious mind.

There is one other feature of automatic script which must be mentioned. Most mediums, whether of the speaking or writing type, usually open up communication by a "control" or "guide" coming through. This control in Miss Cummins' case calls himself Astor. What is the nature or status of a "control" is not definitely known. The control invariably claims to be a discarnate person who is acting as a kind of protector or director of the communication process, and he may be the sole communicator through the medium, although he may convey messages from others with whom he claims to be in touch. On the other hand he may relinquish control of the medium to a direct communicator. In some cases the "control" seems to be a secondary personality of the medium, but there is no point in discussing the technical possibilities here.

In a letter dated November 28th, 1953 Miss Cummins sent me some automatic script which she had obtained while holding a sample of my handwriting in her left hand. In her accompanying letter she wrote to me:

"I tried to get something from your letter in automatic writing. I fear it is all nonsense. I have been overburdened with work lately, so I was tired, and I expect the enclosed is a complete failure. If so, please tear it up and forget it."

The full automatic script which she enclosed is presented below.

"Astor is here. This man's soul is of great interest to me. It is different from that of most people because his deeper mind is receptive to a certain other-World Group. He is in one sense a medium without knowing he is a medium. He has in fact connecting links with Frederic's group – F. W. H. M. who wrote through you. Frederic's group is very concerned because their Society gives them no opening, no opportunity to convince, to impress people with the truth. But they found in this man Johnson a tool, and it is their influence that led him to write his book about the imprisoned soul. They are pleased with what he has done.

"This letter is drawing somebody now. I get a name Charles, also Edward and Rachel: now all this goes. I cannot hold it because another influence comes, someone very eager who pushes back others. A man who, when on earth had a higher nature that gave him supreme moments of understanding. I think he had glimpses of eternity while in the body, or rather what is called mystical experience. They were very sacred and private. He was not able to describe them. He was afraid of entrusting what was of great value to him to others. They might have sneered and scoffed at what meant so much to him, or thought him eccentric. He was some kind of official. He administrated. The work to earn his daily bread was of no interest to him. What mattered was his secret life. After one early mystical experience he longed for more, and it was the study of all that pertained to that divine level of living that engrossed him when he had time in later life. He died during the war sometime in the middle of it. But he was not in it. He worked and lived in Australia. I see him in a big town with a very fine beautiful harbour. I must try and get his name. He shows me the letters Electron. He says it is a foreign word. It is Greek and means Amber. Now he shows me a rose. I see what he means: his name is AmberRose. He makes a little fish, a Sprat. Amberose Prat. He cuts off the sign of S. He makes it clear his name was Amberose Pratt.

"He says the writer of this letter you hold was a friend of his, or at least he found in him much understanding of the one thing that mattered most to him – all that related to this other-world life and consciousness.

"He says to tell R. C. J. that on earth the body to a great extent controls the mind. Whereas here the mind of the individual controls the body. That is the difference.

"Amberose cannot hold on longer but he wants to get the message through that R. C. J. wrote a book of which, though it has minor faults, he wholly approves. For it is true so far as truth can go on earth at present. Because of his talks with R. C., Amberose Pratt would like him to know this 'On a very high level the sense of separateness vanishes in an all-embracing unity'. It is only at rare times he has had that sublime experience in his present life. But in the light of his greater knowledge he says that what R. C. J. wrote about mystical experience was the best part of the book. He says he was at R. C.'s elbow at the time and gave him some help with it. Amberose is a little remote. I cannot get more from him now except one last message: Death is the beginning of Life.

"I think he died about nine or ten years ago. He did not live to any great age. It was difficult for him to come – only his great desire to reach R. C. led him to make a search for a psychic light. He can make contact with his friend's unconscious self, the greater self which is over here of which R. C. is but a small part. It is that mind discarnate belonging to R. C. that led Amberose to help in this book and perceive it."

I should like to say here that all the statements made about Ambrose Pratt are correct. On January 10th, 1954 I wrote to Miss C. thanking her for this script, assuring her that it was very far from nonsense, and that I should be grateful if she would try again sometime to make contact. Before doing so, I asked her to read a letter addressed to Ambrose, which I enclosed in the envelope. This asked him a number of questions, and I said that I supposed he would be able to read the questions from her mind, and answer them through her automatic script. I should add that I asked Miss C. a number of questions about this first communication, and in particular whether she had any recollection whatever that the name Ambrose Pratt could have been mentioned in conversation when we visited her. In her reply dated January 22nd, she said:

"I am very pleased and surprised to hear that the script I sent really meant something to you. It came with some difficulty and very slowly, so I feared it was subconscious invention. When we met that afternoon the only personal thing I recollect being said was Mrs Johnson telling me she came from Northern Ireland, and that you all stayed for a while this past Summer in her native Co. Donegal,[1] also that you had been staying with relatives in Lancashire. I have no recollection of any mention of the names Ambrose Pratt. I should imagine it would be extremely unlikely that you would have, with that in view, mentioned the name of a great friend. The names came with great difficulty and

[1] This is an error of Miss Cummins' memory. Her *native* county is Co. Down.

only by pictures. I wondered afterwards whether the surname was Fish or Fisher because I kept seeing a small fish, and then a pile of small fishes or sprats. Sprat – I see quantities of them every summer off the Irish coast. But the writing worked it out into Pratt. Names are the most difficult to get through, especially when there is no sitter present."

My wife and I discussed on several occasions whether it was possible that either of us had, in the course of general conversation with either Miss Cummins or her two friends who were present on the occasion of our visit, mentioned Ambrose Pratt or any facts about him. A clear memory of conversation which had taken place about three months earlier is not something that either of us would lay claim to. We have no recollection of this, but since the possibility is one to be considered, I regard it as proper to mention it. Although there are some things in the Astor-script which I do not think would have been mentioned *if* we had mentioned Ambrose in conversation, I do not base my belief that my old friend has been in touch with me on this particular script and its factual information. I base it on the total impression made upon my mind by the substance and characteristics of the later scripts.

I received later a second automatic script from Miss C. dated March 21st, 1954. Whereas the first one had been wholly Astor: in this one he relinquished the pen after an introductory sentence, ostensibly to Ambrose. There was a marked change of handwriting. Astor wrote with a large hand: "Ambrose" wrote smaller. It seemed to me that the latter handwriting was not markedly different from Miss C.'s normal handwriting, although not quite identical with it. I do not attach any weight, however, to the handwriting characteristics; the mechanism is so little understood.

"Astor yes. Amberose Pratt is waiting for the pen and I will help him to write directly to his friend."

(Change of handwriting)
"Ambrose.
"My dear Raynor,
        "I have been far from you these many years and it is a matter of thankfulness and joy for me to be permitted at last to write to you with the help of the daemon Astor. I must try and be as brief as possible and not waste this opportunity today as I have a direction to give you.
        (1) I want you to realise that there is design in everything. The time was not ripe for me to break the long silence before I was called from

fairer realms than you can ever possibly imagine or faintly conceive as long as you are in the flesh. This in order to act as a liaison officer. A group of scholars, those mentioned in the previous message, required me to be their link with you in order to give you a certain direction. I may tell you that you are being used for a purpose. But you have freedom of choice and can reject the first task I shall proceed to suggest. Indeed you can reject any task that may be presented to you later.

"Occasionally the F. W. H. Myers group which I shall henceforth call the Group have conveyed ideas to your deeper mind, or the general impulse that led you for instance to write *The Imprisoned Splendour*. Now to prove to you that what I am saying to you is true, I must tell you that they have directed you of recent times to study Douglas Fawcett's philosophic works. In their view the one weakness in your own book was the philosophic section in it. Your finest achievement was that part which dealt with Mysticism. Your subconscious received a telepathic message which helped to lead you on through another to Fawcett's work.

"The modern evidence presented in the experimental work of Psychical Research is a base or foundation on which to build or paint a constructive picture of the Life to come. I am putting this crudely and to express it bluntly the Group require of you another book, and the structure based on psychical research evidence is *Imaginism*. Fawcett by a stroke of supreme genius has obtained the answer, so far as any man may, to the various riddles that haunt the minds of seekers after truth, conceiving God as Divine Imagination, in the whole bold conception presented in his two notable books of *Dialogues*. It is of the first importance that you, a scientist, should come out as a disciple of Fawcett and make known his ideas. It is the philosophy of the future – of an era of reconstruction after the long destruction of the past half century. In such a book you can of course add to and build on the Fawcett philosophy plus the Psychical Research evidence plus Mysticism.

"Men do desire and are gropingly seeking, the Group tells me, for a fresh interpretation of the World system that harmonises with modern knowledge, and this, neither the accepted creeds nor academic philosophy are able to supply. Fawcett's philosophy reinforced by your scientific knowledge and your knowledge of the experimental work in psychical research, might well reconcile religion and science, put an end to their long conflict, and deal a fell blow to scientific materialism. You see, Fawcett's work offers a new and original outlook on the

I

Cosmos, based on metaphysical argument, is sound and straight-forward, and to a great extent intelligible to the reader not trained in philosophy. Fawcett's books were written before recent developments in psychical research, so he has under-estimated its value as a base or foundation of an empirical character for his philosophical ideas. That, and no proper appreciation of the higher aspects of Christianity are the weaknesses in his books, but these are minor points. On the main and essential points, I, a traveller in eternity who has had further and amazing mystical experiences since leaving Earth, can assure you of the rightness of Fawcett's views. He demonstrates how useless are such concepts as that of the Absolute. He reconciles man's own innate sense of the freedom of the will with a Cosmos that is not so determinate in character as Science would have it. He has provided a satisfactory solution of the riddle of Evil, and clarified ideas on Time. Above all, in constructive thought he excels. I can assure you of the truth of his showing how from Divine Imagination are born the World-systems containing the centres of consciring that are to act for themselves as free agents, limited only by the source from which they spring. Now Fawcett is a very old man; his works are little known. The Group who have asked me to present you today with the conception of a new book desire you to be the disciple or apostle of Fawcett. You are of course in such a new book to add to the vision of Imaginism your own original thought and fresh knowledge, and the Group will endeavour to help you in this respect. Fawcett's is the vision splendid, built up as it can be, on psychical research and mysticism.

"This task offered to you is more important than anything else, so I beg of you to give it your serious consideration. There is only a little power left to deal with the points you raised in your letter. . . ."

The questions which I had asked Ambrose, which were of the nature of personal advice, were answered sensibly and briefly. I shall not record these because they have no general interest.

This most remarkable script gave me profound food for thought. It was forceful, authoritative and direct in its style: the work of a critical mind and intellect, offering me certain assurances, and inviting me (not abusing the position to *command* me) to do a task that had never crossed my mind. I knew nothing of a philosopher called Fawcett or his work. The name was vaguely familiar as that of an explorer who was lost on one of his expeditions. (Colonel Fawcett was in fact an older brother of Douglas Fawcett.) The statement in the third paragraph of the script that the Group "have directed you of recent times to study Douglas Fawcett's philosophic works" was itself rather staggering. It was clearly a reference to the fact that a few weeks previously, I had received a letter signed "D. Fawcett". The name meant nothing special to me: but the writer had read *The Imprisoned Splendour* and was writing an appreciative note of this book. He enclosed in this letter, however, a publisher's leaflet printed to advertise Fawcett's two books, *The Zermatt Dialogues*, and *Oberland Dialogues*. He had written in his own hand on this leaflet, "I think these would interest you. They are a meeting point of East and West." So it was true that my attention had been drawn to Fawcett's work! I feel confident that Douglas Fawcett wrote this note spontaneously, and that he and I and possibly my wife, were the only persons on Earth who knew it existed.

Anyone who has had experience of the usual productions of the subconscious mind, will recognise that the style of writing in this script is utterly different from the usual character of these. I wrote of course to Miss C. thanking her and asking if she would tell me what acquaintance if any, she had with Douglas Fawcett. The essential part of her reply is given below, dated April 12th, 1954.

"I think I had better tell you straight away, the extent of my acquaintance with Douglas Fawcett. He lived in Switzerland before the War, and I met him two or three times in the late nineteen-thirties when he was on a visit to London. This led me to read his book *The Zermatt Dialogues*. It greatly impressed me. So in 1939 as I felt I would like to acquire his just published very expensive *Oberland Dialogues* I asked the Editor of *Light* to let me review it. I wrote a short review for *Light* that was published in it in 1940. After that D. F. and his philosophy dropped completely out of my mind as all my energies were absorbed in other work owing to the war, etc. I did not meet Douglas Fawcett again until about three years ago. He had married again, and what led to our meeting was my biography of E. O. E. Somerville the authoress of *The Irish R. M.* etc. and Ireland's greatest story teller. Mrs Fawcett was much interested in my biography as she had met the Somervilles. So I went to tea with her and her husband. Then we did not meet for some time as is the way in London where one gets so busy.

"Now Douglas Fawcett's brother is the famous S. American explorer Col. Percy Fawcett. He made expeditions into the hinterland of Brazil in search of an alleged pyramid and ruined city. From the last expedition he and his eldest son did not return. A number of years ago,

I received in automatic writing from Col. Percy Fawcett, a rather curious and interesting account of his adventures and of how he and his son died. The early part of the narrative was in certain facts corroborated, but his end remains a mystery. Miss Gibbes [a close friend of Miss C.] sent a copy of the book to an old friend Sir David Russell. He was much interested, and last year when *Exploration Fawcett* a life of Col. Fawcett, was published by his son Brian, Sir David wrote to me and urged that my psychic record purporting to come from Col. Fawcett should be published. I said I must first show it to a relative. Of the family I only knew his brother Douglas, so I got in touch with him. He was much interested in the Percy Fawcett script, and asked me to give him a sitting in order that he might talk to his brother Percy. Poor Percy F. was rather crowded out, and most of the writing at the two sittings came I think from a Prof. Keightley and G. R. S. Mead and the Group.

"But of one thing you can be absolutely assured, I deliberately refrained from mentioning you or *The Imprisoned Splendour* for a reason."

Miss C. then mentioned in confidence, why she is certain that neither myself nor my book was mentioned between them at this meeting – and I accept this. She continues in the letter:

"I think this about covers my connection with Douglas Fawcett. But you see I do know his books. On the other hand I am completely untrained in philosophy, and I have never been to a University. . . . When I obtained the last writing from A. P., Douglas Fawcett was certainly not in my conscious mind. The script was written very rapidly and I had a very vague impression of it until I read it over afterwards. I certainly had no idea that Douglas Fawcett had communicated with you by letter."

Miss Cummins' reference to her meeting with D. F. is independently supported by a letter which the latter wrote to me, dated Dec. 24th, 1953 in which he said:

"Some fortnight ago Miss Cummins received a message from Myers asking her to communicate with me and arrange a meeting. I was away at the time when rung up, but last afternoon had a long sitting with her with script purporting to come from Myers, Keightley, Lord Balfour, my brother (the Brazilian explorer of *Operation Fawcett*), and my first wife. Myers said that their group was extremely interested in Imaginism which is 'nearest the truth' sought by Philosophy, and will be the philosophy of the future. Advice was given and I was urged to publish two new books: a volume of *Letters to a Graduate* and my *Epic of Life* (poetry), almost completed. My first wife reminded me of what actually occurred during a motor tour in Italy in 1928. She died at a hotel on the lake Maggiore and I drove the car with her dead body to Domodossola where the body was embalmed, incinerated later at Lausanne, and the ashes thrown (as she had wished) into Lake Leman. Now Sir, is all this Miss Cummins' unconscious mind (irreflective consciring), or is it communication with another world level? I am unable at present to decide. Douglas Fawcett."

At the time of production of the March 21st script from Ambrose Pratt there is no indication that either D. F. or Miss C. was aware that the other had written to me. I have quoted D. F.'s letter, however, to show that the Myers Group were becoming active in December, 1953, and that at the time of the March 21st script, ideas about Imaginism and D. F.'s work had been stirred up in Miss C.'s mind. The question which was now agitating my own mind, after the first staggering impact of the March 21st script, was whether it was to be taken at its face value as a communication from my old friend Ambrose Pratt, or whether Miss Cummins' subconscious mind had been busy somewhat as follows. "Douglas Fawcett's philosophical books have not sold well and he must be rather disappointed. Johnson wrote a book which sold well. He would be the person to popularise Fawcett's ideas, and his old friend Ambrose Pratt might well be the prestige-figure who could convey this idea to him." I did not seriously think this was true, but I felt bound to weigh it as a possibility, and in a letter to Miss Cummins I mentioned this as clearly and tactfully as possible, saying, "Now if only my friend Ambrose would find a sensitive, not known to you, not known to D. F. and not known to me, and instruct this sensitive to send to Johnson, Queen's College, Melbourne, even one significant sentence, this would be a satisfactory proof of the origin of the script." Along with this letter to Miss Cummins, I enclosed another one addressed to Ambrose and asked her to read it before again attempting contact with the other side. In order to save space I shall not reproduce this here. It was warm and cordial and I accepted the task which the Group had asked me to undertake. I invited Ambrose to tell me about his own further mystical experiences; I asked him what were his links with the Myers Group; I asked for advice about meditation, and whether I had any faculty myself for automatic writing, etc.

Having now decided to undertake the task of expounding Imaginism I realised it was time to inform Douglas Fawcett of the extraordinary script of March 21st from Miss Cummins, and let him know that I was hoping to undertake this task. I wrote along these lines to him on April 5th, 1954. On June 1st, 1954 I received another automatic script from Miss Cummins.

"Astor is here. Yes Pratt is coming if you will wait for a little while. Very well I shall tell him to respect the postman and try to write in a small hand."

(Change of handwriting)
"Ambrose Pratt.
"My dear Raynor, or should I say, my dear Thomas,
"I entirely appreciate and applaud your attitude of doubt. But may I call your attention to a few facts that you have possibly overlooked. When I first wrote to you I gave my name, my principal interest during my earthly life – in other words, the secret life, all-absorbing, of the mystic, the occupation which earned my daily bread, an estimate of the time that has flowed away since I left the world of space-time, and lastly, there was mention of our intimate friendship. I considered such identification sufficient, for I was eager to get on with the real task that led me to come from the farther regions of spirit life.

"I told you there was design, and by that I meant that the souls of human beings travelled in groups and the members of each group are inter-related and make a pattern. Discarnate and incarnate souls belong to a group. Though individualised on the earth-plane and seemingly isolated units, on the deeper level they share a common unconscious.

"In this sphere I am a member of the Group-soul to which belong Gurney, Myers, Verrall, Sidgwick, Dixon, and in its higher centres certain mystics. These latter are no longer concerned with the world of men. But those I have named are still passionately concerned with it. On the incarnate level you, this medium (G. C.), R. J. Campbell, Weatherhead, Fawcett, and others belong to this Group-soul. When the earth-time is ripe there has to be a move forward in the design or pattern. You were used by GMVS in order to forward the uncompleted design or work they left behind on earth and you wrote *The Imprisoned Splendour* through and for them. So far so good. But then, to use a simile, you stood at cross-roads and you were in doubt as to what to do next, and intuitively aware that there were gaps in your knowledge. You were consciously aware that you needed further material if you were to write another book. There was the danger of your straying off and devoting yourself to furthering the work you observed at Oxford. The GMVS or Myers' section of our Group-soul brought G. C. forward. I used her, and perforce used the information in the unconscious necessary to compel you immediately to acquaint yourself with Fawcett's books. As earth-time goes there was no time to lose, for you are now in your prime, and more important still, after a decade of destruction in the world of Thought and the world of Action, men and women hunger for reconstruction, not merely materially but spiritually. They revere the scientist. You are at present the only scientist who is a suitable instrument to be used for the purposes of the Myers section of the Group, our Group.

"Of course I used the G. C. memories in the subconscious as far as was necessary, in order to make you act at once and set your feet on the right path. I had previously sufficiently identified myself by conveying to you facts unknown to G. C. What more do you want?

"What we want is that you furnish your mind immediately with the new material and then write this all-important book. The years pass quickly, and the need for it in the world of men increases daily. At present you are the best instrument for our purposes. But if you fail us we shall seek another. I know that you will not fail. I have guaranteed to the Myers' section of the Group that you will succeed, dear friend.

"By all means if you wish, seek confirmation through another medium or mediums, as I think you are doing. But whatever you do or do not, my dear fellow, keep this long book, this *magnum opus* in your mind. Let it germinate for a while, or in other words devote a few minutes of each day, preferably the evening just before sleep to reflection on it, and perhaps make notes if ideas come to you."

After this, follow answers or comment on the more personal questions which I had put to him. On June 20th, 1954 following receipt of this script, I wrote again to Ambrose (per Miss C.) explaining that I would like the last doubt in my mind removed, outlining how this doubt arose and pointing out that if he, Ambrose would take the initiative and find another medium through which to send a significant sentence, this would suffice. I asked a number of questions, the nature of which will be sufficiently clear from the answers given in the following script. This was dated August 17th, 1954.

"Astor is here. Yes Raynor's letter has drawn Ambrose here. He is waiting for the pen. You must understand that spiritually he has travelled far from the world of men and now lives on the fourth plane[1] occasionally penetrating higher still, so he is very detached from the life of earth."

(Change of handwriting)

"Ambrose Pratt.
"Best of friends,
        "It is good to have this letter from you and to feel your nearness in every line of the writing: it brings back memories of our talks and when we laughed together. Only you and an order from my Group-soul could bring me back to what is now to me like an underground region in which like a worm blindly grubbing in the earth I sought you and found you. But I could not have found you if there had not been what I might call a vibratory light. You met this sensitive, and then Ambrose was no longer the worm, he became a glow-worm. I must use the paltry images of language to convey what I mean, though you cannot conceive the joy that luminous glow brought to me in finding you.

"You write of a last 10% of doubt which you demand should be removed. From my point of view I should be doing you a wrong to remove it. Should there not be a ten per cent of faith in your composition? It would be enough to leaven the whole lump. I leave it to you to find the answer to this question. I take it the reply is in the negative, so I am prepared to be the blindworm grubbing further in the clay of earth, but on certain conditions. There has to be a something to light the lamp of the worm. In other words, no one of us can communicate unless that something that ignites is found, unless you make an effort on your part to bring about the opportunity for me to speak through another sensitive. The sensitive in question has to be on a high vibratory measure. I suggest that to such a sensitive you convey through a second party some object that I possessed when on earth – even a few lines of my handwriting would be in my rhythm or the rhythm of my earthly life-line. The second party need not take the object to the sensitive. This second in our duel with doubt should give the object to a stranger, who takes it to the sensitive, then, God willing, I may get the message through to you which is your wish. Immediately or soon after death

[1] Probably a reference to Myers' classification given in Geraldine Cummins' book *The Road to Immortality*.

I might have got through to you in the manner you require, as I was still on what one might call the semi-physical rhythm. But for ten years I have been on the high mystical adventure, and engaged on work for others. . . .

"You ask me what are my chief interests. I have two interests beyond any others. (i) The high mystical adventure. Such experiences are only granted me when I have earned them by hard and sometimes painful work – work for creation which sometimes leads me into a region of shadows – work among the little souls of a lower primitive order – primitive and therefore antipathetic to myself. (ii) My second interest is an aspiration which can only be eventually attained through tremendous effort. I seek to become a member of the Divine Hierarchy of Souls who maintain and conserve the material universe. It is but one among the universes. My dear R. C. the magnitude of creation is inconceivable. Yes, I am always looking forward, but progress is wave-like. One must travel downwards in order to go upwards.

"Yes, so far as my knowledge goes, there is chance within the pattern of life for each individual. Banish from your mind the false superficial idea labelled determinism or fatalism. Within limits each human being has the choice. Only the Spirit of the Group-Soul knows from weighing and balancing his character what choice he is almost certain to make. Secondly, your past life and your progress in it determine some of the events and conditions you meet in your next life. Through your failures you sow the seeds of certain temptations you have to meet again often in very different guises and circumstances. But always there is the element of freewill. It depends on your spiritual and imaginative progress in that particular life what material is necessary not merely to you but to those in your pattern in the following life. Sometimes there are innocent victims of ghastly tragedies on earth. These are occasionally caused by others in your pattern who have not made progress, who have gone backwards. We are members one of another, is indeed a true saying. The hermit or yogi has not sufficiently realised this vital fact when he seeks only his personal salvation. But within the limitations I have briefly and inadequately mentioned we are free. So far as my knowledge goes, the 'Eternal Now' in which all events inhere is a false trail. There is not power enough now to go into this question.

"Bear at least in mind that the initiative of the individual counts, as I have described. But destiny in your present earth-life is made already to a considerable extent for you. The high fences you have to jump or recoil from or take a toss, are there, but you have freewill in the manner in which you negotiate them. That manner affects future events for you in Eternity. Bear in mind above all that God is living, not finished – a static pillar of salt like Lot's wife. He is first and last a Creator, therefore He is creative of Himself, adding to His measure and to eventual bliss all the little souls. Dismiss from your mind the idea of a Spiritual Absolute. I hope to drop thoughts into your Unconscious: in fact I shall do so soon. They concern the book about to be born."

At this point it is appropriate to pause and return to the question raised earlier: are these scripts what they purport to be, or are they creations of Miss Cummins' subconscious mind? My own answer is quite clear. The style of writing in these scripts is very competent, critical and authoritative. Observe the critical comment on the strengths and weaknesses both of my own book and of Fawcett's books. Note the authoritative element: "I can assure you of the truth of his showing how from Divine Imagination are born the World-systems containing the centres of consciring that are to act for themselves as free agents, etc." Observe in the third script of June 1st a courteous and patient rebuke of my scepticism with its satisfying fuller explanation. Note also its accurate diagnosis of my own mood after writing *The Imprisoned Splendour*. Note also the very generous offer in the script of August 17th to be the worm "grubbing further in the clay of earth" to give me the proof I wanted. All this made me convinced that my friend Ambrose was indeed making contact through Miss Cummins. I do not suppose for a moment that Miss C.'s subconscious mind did not at times intrude thoughts and ideas – but by and large, I am satisfied that she was incapable of originating the scripts as a whole. After a good deal of consideration I therefore declined the offer which Ambrose made to give me the satisfaction of "proof" through the use of another medium. There are many subtle features in the scripts which are reminiscent of my friend. The use of the Socratic term "daemon" Astor is typical – and I shall point out others later. The commonly used term is "guide" or "control".

Through the kindness of Miss Cummins these automatic scripts arrived at intervals of a few months over a period of several years. The last was in July, 1960 when Miss Cummins indicated that the demands made upon her by a variety of matters made it necessary for her to curtail this psychic work. The procedure was as indicated before. I would write a letter to my friend Ambrose and send it to Miss Cummins. She would read this before trying for further script. I want to stress again that I do not regard these scripts as "verbal inspiration" I regard the subconscious mind of the sensitive as telepathically receptive of the ideas of Ambrose Pratt but providing to some degree the language expressing them. At the same time, I am bound to say that particularly in one script which I shall present later, dealing with mystical experience which Ambrose had experienced on "the other side" he has managed to reproduce the lyrical and exciting quality of his own style. It is naïve to suppose that passing over the bridge of death makes any immediate difference to a person except probably in the availability of certain powers of the mind – both perceptive and motor. The foolish man does not become any wiser, the evil man any better, the aesthetically insensitive person any more sensitive. I had said to my wife long before this channel of communication opened up, "If there is anyone with whom I should like to make a contact on the other side, it would be Ambrose Pratt. With his wide interests and acute mind, one would surely hear something of interest, and not listen to the clap-trap or moral uplift so characteristic of the general run of alleged communications." I consider myself fortunate in that this wish was granted.

I do not wish to load this essay with too much of the script material, but I think that many who have read so far may like to hear further observations of my remarkable friend. Most of his observations were stimulated by questions I put to him. Some were not. I shall omit purely personal material except where I can point out its evidential value. A great deal of what he passed on is his considered judgment after some ten years or more on the other side, and it should be of general interest. To save space I shall not reproduce my letters to him. My questions will be evident from the nature of his answers.

5th Script dated 10th June, 1955

"Astor comes. Yes, the mystic has been patiently waiting for this opportunity to write."

"Ambrose Pratt.

"I am touched by your saying that you feel profoundly grateful to me. It is a feeling that I do not in the least deserve. I longed to speak to you at an earlier time. But I was only permitted to break the long silence in the appropriate season. In other words, the Group-soul

71

creates the pattern for those who are members of it. It was designed that I should set you a certain task when you, in the measure of earth-time, were ripe for it. So in the years between I might not bring to life the beauty of our old friendship. Of course you might have rejected the task, but if you had done so it would have been to your own loss in the slowing up of the evolution of your own self. There is freewill, there is always the choice. Each unit in the Group-soul can fail or succeed in weaving what is the part designed for him in the projected outline of the embroidered tapestry. You have so far responded and are pulling in the stitches of your fragment according to the imaged conception of the Spirit of the Group. Some time has I believe passed since I last wrote to you. It was considered necessary for a while that you should work alone independently. Now I may again break the silence and I am all eagerness to answer your questions.

"Yes, the Group-soul contains many souls. Ours is one of those which corresponds to the term 'sub-imaginal field' which is used in his books by our friend D. F. You ask is the number of the Group-soul being added to? The reply is in the affirmative. There is no evolution of a fixed number, for the number to a great extent depends on the response made by the members of the Group in fulfilling or failing to fulfil their part in the imaged pattern.

"The Spirit of the Group-soul is that with which I communicate in mystical experiences. But it depends on myself how far it may lead me into a higher synthesis . . . through grace I might say, for many are my shortcomings still.

"The Divine Hierarchy of souls who maintain the material universe: are they individual beings who have finally evolved to this level or perfected Group-souls? They are both. A member of the Divine Hierarchy is one and yet many. The inspiring Spirit makes these souls one. It consists of many individual beings who have evolved to this level, but they are contained as it were within one of the Divine Hierarchy of Souls. On earth man lives on a low level of consciousness. But it has been recognised that even man is a poly-psychic being. Eventually you will be one of the individual beings within a perfected Group-soul. But your consciousness then has changed, widened, expanded immeasurably.

"Wisdom, Love, Beauty and Goodness are the supreme values for me now. Myers has truly written that God is greater than Love. He is Wisdom such as transcends anything that man can imagine. But Wisdom might be said to be the directive that can and does inspire

Love, Beauty, and Goodness in flashes according to the level and limitations of the soul.

"Astor is both a secondary personality of Miss Cummins, and an individual who once lived on earth."

(Now follows a critical discussion of a passage in one of D. F.'s books, which Ambrose says should be qualified or more clearly explained. I will not introduce this here.)

"Though the Spirit (of a Group-soul) cannot be said to limit itself by incarnation, yet it functions in man when he summons it. The Spirit may be described as a pervading Light from above, that can, though it rarely does lighten up the dark ordinary ego of man. But primitive men who were wholly physical, wholly the creatures of their bodies, perished at death. These were experiments and early failures of a sub-imaginal field or fields. Not by any means all among highly evolved men obtain the guerdon of immortality. Bear in mind that innumerable experiments are made and that some are failures. There is variety, there is no inflexible law. . . ."

6th Script dated 12th Nov., 1955
"Astor is here. Wait for a while and Ambrose will write."

"Ambrose Pratt.
"My dear friend, more than friend, brother-initiate in a far time,
"It is not strange, it is inevitable in view of our past, that you should sit down at your desk in Queen's College and write to me, neither is it strange that I should reply to your letter. As an old country-woman once wisely said, 'Miracles are easy when you know how to work them.' It is not the conscious mind that knows. The knowledge resides in the Spirit of the Group-soul. But the miracle cannot be worked unless the conscious mind desires it strongly, vehemently. Even so there is often delayed action, for the pattern or design in the Imaginal Field is of the first importance. After my passing you longed to have a sign or some news of me. But the time was not ripe for the weaving of the pattern as you will realise yourself. Neither you nor the times were ready. Action had to be delayed. But the desire for news of me remained latent in your consciousness. That faithful love eventually worked the miracle. But you could have failed even then, you could have refused the task set you. In that sense you had freewill and could have refused the weaver's work in the pattern

offered against the creative principle, and put back to another earth-life the fulfilment of a design in the tapestry of time.

"Long ago, you and I and Douglas Fawcett were, as I have perceived, initiates under a bond of secrecy at Eleusis. Some day I may be permitted to relate some part of our story – convey fragments from the record of that epoch. In this present life, as philosopher, mystic, and scientist, we were the natural and needed development of that distant life in Greece. I use the verb 'needed', and by that I mean necessary for the part we are to weave in the design, and in fact have been weaving; obeying the Imaginal Field, or, as is popularly called Fate, not resisting the creative impulse, the great opportunity to introduce Novelty into the Design.

"I want you to realise the importance of your share in the weaving of this pattern. You are the scientist. In the view of educated people of the 20th century, you are therefore the prophet who speaks with authority. You are in a position denied to the philosopher and mystic. The inspired philosopher who is not a professor at a university beset by conventional doubts and fears, can get no hearing from the educated public. The mystic is in their view a deluded fool betrayed by his complexes. It was fitting therefore that I should be promoted and direct the design from this sphere at the time appointed. You have been given the heaviest task of all. You are the spear-head that makes the direct frontal attack on a colossal scholastic dogma and cynicism. I think I can promise you that your book will arouse cold rage and thereby scoffing and scornful dismissal in certain quarters. But the learned Pharisees are eventually defeated by the Sun of time, and the needs of the times. The need is there – is urgent. In Milton's phrase, 'The hungry sheep look up and are not fed.' Our book will initiate the awakening, the resurrection from scientific materialism. Very slowly no doubt, it will have a powerful influence on the world of thought. Within it reside the seeds that will eventually flower in a new transforming religion. You must have no doubts: you must not at any time allow yourself to be discouraged. . . . Imaginism belongs to no church. It reconciles East and West. It has an appeal that is world-wide for thinking people. It will in time dethrone scientific agnostical doubt. Though so far as I can see you live the full span of life, you will not witness its complete effects upon mankind. I think that the leaven works very gradually, so do not be disappointed by initiatory results of your work. God's time is not man's time.

"By the way, Fawcett's treatment of Time solves the problem of

Time – is the correct solution. His destruction of the idea of the Spiritual Absolute is of primary importance in the re-creation of a true religion for thinking people. . . .

"As you have I think, fully realised, the Chapter named Birth and Death in *Oberland Dialogues* is of importance because of its supreme interest for the educated public. See that you present its ideas clearly and simply. F. W. H. M. has drawn my attention to a few paragraphs in his essay on the Subliminal Mind in *The Road to Immortality*. He says that he tried to convey in it an idea that was later effectively developed by D. F. Here is what the latter wrote:

" 'But this divine Imaginal Field is to be lit by finite centres of consciring who will exist not only for God but also for themselves. At first the regions in which these centres will arise are only tracts of content, some more or less simple, some complex, etc.' Chapter: Birth and Death.

"Here is the F. M. paragraph in *The Road to Immortality*. It says:

" 'The larger mind has been there in a state unformed from the dark ages, etc.' You may read on and you will see that D. F. puts more explicitly what F. M. sought to convey. Compare the 'larger mind unformed' with D. F.'s 'tracts of content,', etc. You will see that it is the same conception. Human beings ask Whence? Whither? This conception, tracts of content, or the unformed larger mind is a correct reply to the question Whence? Fawcett may not like the suggestion, but F. W. H. M. conveyed the general idea of this chapter Birth and Death to him. . . ."

The reader may be interested in my own reactions to parts of this script. The statement that Fawcett, Pratt and myself were linked in a former life in ancient Greece interested me, for I accept the idea of reincarnation as a thoroughly reasonable one with much to commend it. But whether in fact this information is true, I personally cannot say. I have no conscious awareness of former lives. The critical acumen and philosophical insight shown in the latter part of the script seem to me (with due respect) quite outside Miss Cummins' normal interests and capacity. If they are not from my old friend Ambrose Pratt, I have no plausible suggestion as to their origin. In a later script dated 22nd January, 1956 technical help is again forthcoming. Ambrose starts:

"My dear Raynor,
        "I have first to convey a message from F. W. H. M. He wishes

to clear up a possible misunderstanding, though indeed words are inadequate for the explanation of such a theme. He says:

" 'When endeavouring to explain the seventh plane in *The Road to Immortality* I spoke of Timelessness as the condition of that state. But the word does not imply that there is no succession of events, no past and future. There is, as Fawcett truly observes, the adding-up of the time-process for the very enrichment of the nature of God.

" 'We must realise (i) The conception of the Eternal in the Creative Imagination (timelessness), (ii) The continuous fulfilling of this conception (succession of events). The dream in the Supreme Artist's imagination of the picture of all Time is static and therefore timeless. The execution of the picture means succession of events. Sometimes they vary and are different from the original conception. In that sense we have duality: Time and Timelessness on the seventh plane.

" 'The Dream of the Eternal is the world of the Spiritual Absolute, the favoured conception of many philosophers. But they have ignored duality and do not admit progression. There is no place in their hypothesis for addition. . . .' "

This kind of material in an automatic or inspired script is totally different from the products of ordinary subconscious mentation. It shows that there was a very active interest being taken, particularly by Ambrose Pratt and Myers in the expository aspect of the book I was writing. Later in this same script Ambrose says:

"You could have refused the task, then I would have been let down, as it was I who told the Myers group that you were the one man, the one scientist who could write it successfully. Then I linked up your creative mind with that of Myers, and it is he who has been inspiring you principally. He recently told me that you were a satisfactory interpreter. But do not think that the connection began with this last book. The Group in a general sense directed you in the writing of *The Imprisoned Splendour*. I told them to try and impress you with the urgent need for such a book. Though in a sense it was your idea, their urgent desire for it stimulated you and gave you the necessary confidence to write and complete it. You will later be given further work."

I may perhaps remark that I had no *conscious* awareness of these contacts or inspiration: but what is inspiration and where does it come from? I have no difficulty whatever in accepting the information. The time came when I had completed the typescript of the book called

Nurslings of Immortality and I sent off one of the copies to Miss Cummins whose generous work as a sensitive had made it possible. Soon afterwards I received a further automatic script dated 6th May, 1956.

"Astor is here and Ambrose is waiting for the pen.

"Ambrose Pratt.
"My dear Raynor,
        "My usual prosaic calm has been shaken and that makes writing difficult. I have had what might be described as a bird's-eye view of your book. We of the Group had a general sense of it, but much escaped us. Through the eyes of this medium I have been able to read it as a reviewer might, and can give an assessment. It is wholly favourable. My dear fellow, you have surpassed yourself. I have presented my report of the M.S. to the Group and its members are satisfied that all they wished said has been said, and that in choosing you as their intermediary or spokesman they have chosen wisely, and I have been asked to convey to you their congratulations and gratitude. It helps to release them from their sense of responsibility towards anxious suffering mankind, so they are grateful. But do not be elated. I must warn you that the book is very provocative and from some quarters will receive sharp criticism. That is our view. It is a superb achievement and for that reason dangerous. You cannot attack academic thought without rousing emotional prejudice. On the other hand many people will welcome the vision and recognise its truth as you have expounded it. . . ."

I must ask the reader to excuse the quoting of these too generous complimentary remarks. I have to confess that a colourful exaggeration was frequently one of the characteristics of Ambrose Pratt's narration. I was glad, however, to have the approval of the finished work by those who invited me to undertake it, and the book certainly seems to have been very significant judging by the letters of those who have written to me after studying it.

I had more than once invited Ambrose to tell me, if he could, what developments had taken place along the line of mystical experience. In a script dated 15th July, 1956 he met my request, and I reproduce the content of this below.

"My dear Raynor,
        "I am glad that you have asked me about my friendship with AE. Not long after my promotion to this life I prayed for a guide who

K

would be master to the pupil, and cause me to rise into the unitive life, attain to the mystical grade. My prayer was granted and because AE was of my time and generation on earth, but a little preceding me, he appeared radiant from the higher levels and became my guardian philosopher. I will pass over the preparation, the conflict, the struggle, which was necessary for the creation of the inner harmony. I shall tell of my first experience which was an interpretation of a little corner of the earth, a vision, a feeling of the Unitive Principle behind Nature in a small fragment of the world of the senses.

"It was an island in the Gulf of Mexico. There the winters are as mild as June in England. The sea about the island is as light and blue as a sapphire. I perceived green pastures, the earth crowned with fruits, groves of cedars, palms and oranges, brilliant but not cruelly burning sunshine, that in the eyes of men apparelled Nature in its gayest colours. Life, swarming life in form is there. I had the sensuous human pleasure of perceiving it all. But how trivial was that pleasure when my mind gradually went inward to the genie. The process might be likened to that of a sea-gull on a cliff with shut wings just before its take-off from a jutting rock. Suddenly the great wings are outspread and it is off, rising, soaring above the immensities of the ocean beneath the wide cirrus-streaked skies. It is a poor simile, but how except objectively can I convey to you the ecstasy of that flight into Union? Then I knew the unity behind the separate myriad forms animated by life on that small island. I was one with the Divine Imagining actively maintaining and conserving that fragment of Nature. I was one with the Artist experiencing the creative rapture that was his, one with the essence, the conception, and containing as well the physical representation, the imaged product of consciring. I was aware of the large, the little, the infinitesimal on that island. I experienced breath of life animating the tiniest coloured insect there; life in orange grove and cedar and tall waving palm; life in the black and white people on the isle; animal existence there. But it came like a chorus, many voices making one earth-time song. I was aware of the whole, of each separately, and of activating creative bliss.

"There is a quotation from the Gospels I then truly apprehended – I have forgotten the exact words – One sparrow shall not fall without your Heavenly Father knowing it. How true that is when you, Raynor, realise that Divine Imagining maintains and conserves all Nature.

"That was my initial experience in this life of Transcendental Unity. It was a first lesson in mysticism for my liberated soul. I have

78

had many other more wonderful experiences since: they were graded according to my progress. Beside me, fusing with me, always was my guardian philosopher: fusing at the peak, separate, instructing, guiding, as we climbed towards that peak.

"The first series of lessons concerned the planet earth from whence I had come. We traversed the Sahara deserts, we visited the poles, we absorbed the human life in great cities. We visited the lonely Himalayas, the Rockies. We went East, West, South, and North perceiving the outer and then experiencing the inner in sections – the essence of each global section preparatory to experiencing the life of earth as one Whole within Transcendental Unity. I visited that sacred country Tibet's sacred centre, that other Northern spiritual centre, the dream-island of Iona. I could write of all these mystical experiences – the peace, the enraptured quiet of the skies above Iona, the particular and the Whole of each centre.

"I rode upon the winds, rode over the waves, leaped the mountains, entered into the dewdrops of the dawn. I saw the conception of each in the essence, so much more exquisite, finer, subtilised. The initiatory conception is a country where beauty has no ebb, decay, no rotting, withering, where Joy is Wisdom, Time an endless melody. Mistakenly I use the verb 'saw', but I experienced it within my whole being. . . . Some other time I may be permitted to tell you of further mystical heights and depths beyond all human knowledge. . . ."

I freely confess that I find this description most fascinating and beautiful and it was quite reminiscent to me of the ability which Ambrose possessed to use language very felicitously. Passages showing the lyrical quality of his style when describing some exquisite natural scene, could be quoted from several of his early books. I found both the substance and the style of this script particularly reminiscent of Ambrose. This style and language is not characteristic of Miss Cummins' writing, and as to its substance, she wrote in a letter accompanying the script, "I was very interested in the account of mystical experience given in the enclosed script. I am afraid I am very ignorant as regards mysticism and have not read Miss Underhill's books. How does this script square with other mystical experiences, I wonder?"

During the following four years, although the main task which led Ambrose Pratt to make contact with me was completed, I was able (through the kindness of Miss Cummins) to keep in touch with him at intervals. I asked him many questions, some of personal interest and some general. I shall therefore select from later scripts the answers he gave to me on matters which may interest my reader.

Some of my readers have possibly delved into, or perhaps studied closely, the writings (usually voluminous) of some of the esoteric cults and schools of thought which are active today. They are many: Theosophy, Anthroposophy, Gurdjieff-Ouspensky, Rosicrucianism, the Arcane School of Alice Bailey, and hosts of others. In this jungle of revelation, clairvoyant perception, and mediumistic recordings, through which a half-obscured stream of ancient wisdom runs, the student who retains independence of judgment must often have wondered what to believe: how to sift the truth from the nonsense. One of the beliefs held by several of these schools is that there are beings who have graduated as it were in the school of man and passed to higher levels, but whose service and concern is still with the human family. They are frequently called "Masters", and some of them are said to live in human bodies, particularly in order to help mankind. I put the question to Ambrose (through a letter read by Miss Cummins):

"Are there in fact 'Masters'? Alice Bailey who founded one such school, wrote voluminously what she claimed to be hearing from a Tibetan Master D. K. I understand that some of her writings are doubtful. Could you give me an opinion on say *The Treatise on Cosmic Fire*. Is it substantially reliable?"

The answer I received dated April 19th, 1957 is as follows:

"Yes, there are a few people living in the Himalayan region, and several in other parts of the world, who have devoted a great part of their lives to special training, which in its first stages led to the development of extraordinary psychic powers of telepathy, clairvoyance, astral travelling, etc. For instance, several yogis can, in rare circumstances, dematerialise their physical bodies and materialise them in another place. These yogis also have mystical experiences.

"But yogis vary very much in regard to their powers. Certain of them, the lesser ones, are called 'Masters'. These are those which certain esoteric schools of thought maintain are using human bodies. But you have to make a sharp division between 'the Word' or inspired teaching – the Word made flesh – and a special power to control the flesh. I do not dispute that a 'Master' in his astral travelling actually appeared to A. Bailey – made himself visible to her. But that is a very much lower or lesser gift than the instruction or teachings imparted.

'By their fruits ye shall know them.' I do not dispute that A. Bailey heard from the Master D. K. and took down all he had to impart and published it. But what is the quality of such writings? Use your own judgment my dear fellow. There are certain truths or partial truths in such books, but on the whole they are, shall we say, rather superficial. They do not come to grips with some of the baffling enigmas that haunt thinkers. I am not properly acquainted with *The Treatise on Cosmic Fire* you mention. I am with others – *The Treatise on White Magic*. I do not on the whole quarrel with its information about training in occultism, but it is elementary.

"Other books from the Master D. K. taken down by A. B. demonstrate that the author D. K. is mistaken in certain material imparted or has not faced up to the problems involved. In other words he is not a Master of Wisdom. By all means read the A. B. books and pick out the grains of gold from the dross. But D. K. shall we say, was not on a very high level of consciring. The work for example of D. Fawcett is on a much higher level of consciring. He is inspired by a Group who never claimed to be Masters, but they have mastered much Wisdom, and though the form may not always be clear, they have conveyed a generally true view in a magnificent conception of the Divine Creativity. Yes, some of the writings of A. B. I have studied are doubtful. You must apply the same critical standards to the writings of 'Masters' as you do to the works of Plato, Plotinus, Fawcett, and other lesser philosophers."

I had asked the question, "Is it possible to convey in words anything of your own environment, the setting of your present life, and the work you are doing?" In the same script, from which I have just quoted he gave me this fragment in reply:

"Of Nature in Australia, I have been lately thinking: of its varied bird life, of those birds I knew a long time ago, of the typical lyre bird, laughing jackass, and emu. I cannot write more now but I may say that I am training to become an organiser of seasonal bird life in connection with the planet earth. I am one of many souls who work at breath of life in regard to birds to be born each spring. The old patterns are conserved and there has to be a collective drive in regard to launching the young of each species every Spring. Another time I shall tell of this creative work if the English language will furnish me, as I fear it won't, with words in which to express its character. Then I shall tell also of my environment."

The chance to amplify this interesting fragment did not come, but I was led to a good deal of interesting speculation as to various forms of artistic and creative activity which may be natural to souls on higher levels of being.

On another occasion I asked a question about reincarnating souls. Do they in successive lives have experience in bodies of both sexes or keep to a body of one sex? I asked also if there was any truth in the old idea of "affinities" who were twin halves as it were of a complete soul who had been separated at an earlier stage.

"The sexual instincts . . . are a powerful force shaping events for each individual, helping to create them for evil or for good in their pilgrimage. But the male and female experience of their bodies is totally dissimilar, that is to say, so different, it is essential for the average individual soul to have both experiences. If a soul is always a man, and another soul is always a woman, then they lose one half of a fundamental experience on the earth level of existence. The vast majority of souls most certainly have male and female experience of a human life otherwise they would be incomplete. (Incidentally, the masculine woman or Lesbian, and the female or homosexual man, are those individuals who have been too extremely masculine or too extremely feminine in their previous incarnations, and have brought with them therefore those characteristics into a body of the opposite sex.) In the case for instance of a soul who has visited the earth five or six times, it may well have had four or five experiences of the masculine or feminine life, but it undoubtedly has to know the two aspects. There is great variety in the number. There may be a balance: two of each aspects. Much depends on the development of the soul and the part it plays in the design of the Imaginal Field. I agree with the idea of affinities in certain cases, but it is not . . . a general rule."

On another occasion, the question had been raised of the difference between real love, which is that of soul for soul, and what is often miscalled love and is but the fascination of one personality by aspects of another. Ambrose said:

"In relation to the problem of physical death, you may ask, was Frederic Myers in error when he called his great book *Human Personality and its Survival of Bodily Death*? My reply is, 'No, he was not mistaken.' I must give you an illustration of what I mean. Suppose a man is separated from his beloved through her early death for a period of fifty years, has she remained static, the young girl he loved in the Hereafter? The reply is No, in the case of an evolving soul. She has gone on to a higher level. But the human personality of the young beautiful girl he knew in life, has not perished: it has merely been discarded and remains near the earth-level. When the man who loves her real self dies, she descends from the higher level and assumes the human personality he knew on earth. His has been a faithful love for the image of the young girl enshrined in his heart, so she appears to him after the shock of death as she was in his memory. There is then for them the renewal and reliving of the ecstasy of their brief youthful love on earth. Thus he who is born as an infant into the Hereafter is gradually educated, as it were, and then through various stages she helps him to evolve to her higher level. When we communicate with men and women on earth we reassume our discarded human personality as it was at death. It is a labour of love or affection. So when all those on earth whom we love have joined us in the Hereafter we do not as a rule put on the old fancy dress of human personality and communicate with men; or we do so only if we have an urgent desire to help or influence men for humanity's benefit.

"There is of course a great number of unevolved souls who remain human personalities living in their desired picture of earth for many years (according to earth-time) on this side of the border. Usually they go no further on the upward way. They eventually reincarnate."

One of the difficulties which the modern scientist and philosopher put forward about survival – if they think about this question at all – is that the survival of human personality without any kind of bodily organism is an absurd notion. In a script dated December 2nd, 1958 this question is dealt with at length.

"For many centuries Hindu occultists have stated that there is no matter. Oddly enough, modern scientists appear to have come to this conclusion also. In fact they abolished matter when they informed us that the universe is a continuum of energy. But energy is invisible to the unassisted senses of man. The fact that his unassisted senses do not perceive certain kinds of energy, including his own energy, does not indicate that man is unconscious, i.e., not having a stream of experience. . . .

"To a post-mortem individual such as I am, these scientists' assertion is a totally false one. They are still in the position of the nineteenth century scientist and think of man as a lump of matter, as a hard billiard ball, and not as energy in a vast continuum of energy of which there are various kinds.

"Immediately after death the man's mind that has left the physical body has a field or appearance, and, as during his life on earth, is functioning on a level of energy that is a different rate of energy from the physical rate. During his life on earth the essence of his mind or qualities has been travelling in a different key and scale from the physical. But the chasm has a bridge. For instance, your directive mind directs the physical body by means of a quasi-physical substance, connecting threads slowing down the mental aspect in order to express itself in a material world. Now there is a replica of the human body of this quasi-physical substance, which has been called the 'double' or body for sleep, in which the higher part of the mind can reside, and in which all that part of it which has been active during the day rests. The gap of sleep enables the higher mind to recharge the physical nervous system and brain with nervous energy. This double is on a differently functioning rate from the man's physical body's rate, to the extent that it is invisible to the human eye or other human perceptions, and it is the immediate form or appearance of the man after death on the post-death level of energy. There is of course a period of adjustment, a breaking away from the quasi-physical by the total of man's mind and memories, during that period named Hades. Christ called it a descent into hell, but that 'hell' was not the meaning of the fire and brimstone hell so ably expounded in the past by certain sadistically minded divines. . . .

"Death means the breaking away of the mental from the slower quasi-physical rate, the sundering from the material world. Man's mind and personality merely travel *in toto* at a more rapid rate on a separate energy, as it were, when resurrected from Hades. Hence the invisible cloak of the fairy-tale. You cannot perceive what is travelling too fast or too slow or in another mode, despite its bodily appearance in that mode. That other world is as real in appearances, in colours, forms and light to the so-called *dead* man's mind as is your present world to you. It might be said to be a continuation of that world but as the energy is travelling in a different mode – is a separate energy from the material earth – it is different in many respects, and is for its appearances more dependent upon the character of the mind of the dead man and of his posthumous circle of souls, than was the earth he has left behind him. The important point to emphasise is that it is a background, and so for him the flow of experience continues. The nursery view of the Western philosopher is that the stream of experience stops with the death of the physical body: that existing in a void, he can no longer exist! If that were the case I would agree with him. But much of the evidence of recent psychical research goes to prove that man on earth is a compound of energy functioning on two levels.

"I will take one illustration out of many, as evidence for this. A human being is functioning on the two levels if he or she is an accurate prophet. What is called the super-conscious mind of man functions more freely on our different energy rate in cases of intuition and in the great number of cases of prevision on record. The human being is strictly speaking not dualistic. The successful medium, automatist, prophet, and even the diviner, are merely functioning on two levels of energy at the same clock time, when they are making experiments. But it is exceedingly difficult to maintain continuously for even an hour or so, work on two modes of energy. Hence the gaps, the errors, the mistakes made in many cases, even in the best work.

"I do not blame the scientist for not recognising the implications of the assertion that the universe is a continuum of energy. They deal only with ponderables, the weighable, the physical, the analysable. They deal with only a fraction of the real world.

"But as I perceive the modern world below its surface there appears a related phenomenon which is the collapse of moral values. Mankind seems to be reverting to the Dark Ages equipped with all the resources of a perverted science. On earth, scientists appear to be regarded as authorities on almost everything. They are not to blame because their discoveries have helped so much to produce the fading out of moral values. . . ."

This important script seems to me to present in terms with which modern man is familiar, an intelligible conception of how, after physical death, a person may find himself in a world every bit as objective as this one.

The next script from which I will quote is interesting comment on, and comparison between, the Eastern or world-negating type of mysticism and the Western or world-affirming type. This comment arose naturally out of the fact that Miss Cummins had received and just read a typescript copy of my book *Watcher on the Hills*. As indicated in an earlier script (p. 145) this fact made it possible for Ambrose to become aware of the book's content in detail. In the next automatic script I was therefore not surprised to receive many useful and critical suggestions in relation to the book. Part of this script I reproduce below. It is dated 26th July, 1958.

"I want some more passages about the religious life as it might be lived by the ordinary man who craves truly for some mystical experience that will help him in what is often the drudgery of living – with its petty worries and mean temptations, its fears – some of them deep fears, in this insecure perilous age, as it appears to many on earth. Indeed for twentieth century man I would add to Our Lord's Prayer, 'Deliver us from fear.' Fear, in some form or another is the root from which grows so much evil. The real mystic is above and beyond all fear, resting within the deep peace of God. But he does not reach that position in most cases unless he has been through much conflict, and experienced many trials. I speak of the ordinary man.

"Here is another point I would like to draw your attention to. On earth during my lifetime, I had certain mystical experiences, and I lived and worked as an ordinary man. That, I am now of opinion is the better way, save in the most exceptional cases, for the mystic. We are born into the world, not to fly from life, but to experience it for at any rate a fair span of the years allotted to us. I have never since my passing regretted the fact that I did not become a contemplative, retiring to a hermitage or monastery in my youth and staying there. Complete withdrawal from the world, renunciation of everything in it, disdain alike of pleasure and pain, the life of the Eastern contemplative, should not be favoured by most mystical seekers, by those who search for the celestial way. I do not approve of the Buddha's saying, 'Men who love nothing in the world are rich in joy and free from pain.' If not in their present earthly life, in another future life, they have to experience joy and pain. Secondly, how very odd is this richness that is without love of a world God has created. The flight to God from the works of God is surely ironical commentary. In Indian metaphysics complete retreat on the part of the mystic from life and the world is, in my opinion, too much emphasised. The mystical experience is most serviceably harvested through sharing, through living a part of one's life in the world, as did Christ. 'Let your light so shine before men.' For the great mystics teach us to practise immortality on earth.

"The greatest of all mystics, Christ, knew and loved the world . . . but Christ was a man of joy, in love with the world because it was the work of God.

"Admittedly there is more than one path for the seeker of Pure

Light to choose from at the outset of his earthly pilgrimage. But the mystic who lives in the world, radiating the joy of his mystical experiences as did Christ, chooses the better part, better than the Indian mystic who sits under a tree, remaining in complete withdrawal from the spurned world, having no love for God's creation – the flowering earth, no love for little children, yet 'of such is the Kingdom of Heaven'.

"I do not throw any doubt on the Buddha's saying that 'Men who love nothing in the world are rich in joy and free from pain.' They do not 'Love thy neighbour as thyself.' It is quite often a very difficult task to love one's neighbour, difficult also to recognise the deep truth of St Paul's saying, 'We are members one of another.' Perhaps I write too satirically. Pray give no heed to what you do not like in the presentation of this view. I would merely suggest that you add to your book some passages that give clear guidance to the average man who wishes to develop himself mystically and religiously.

"The Group maintain that you have done so in your remarkably fine last chapter. In their view it embodies remarkably all that should be said in guidance, and they warmly congratulate you. . . . But my dear Raynor, it comes right at the end of the book. Will the average reader wait for his guidance until he reaches the final chapter? . . . The members of the Group consider chapter nine of especial value to the intellectual. F. Myers is particularly pleased with it, and says it is masterly. The blend of soul with spirit may be regarded as the highest achievement of man. Behind all the shifting changes of human personality is that gradually growing permanent and everlasting self – a self the psychologists do not recognise or in any way admit. Brain-wash a man, reduce him to apparent idiocy: it is only the outward personality that is thus disintegrated, the permanent self remains whole, untouched. But I digress. You are right, F. M. says in your brief analysis of madness. F. M. is pleased that you have made clear that many mystical experiences are of the spirit of the Group-soul; as you say, 'The primary and fundamental type of mystical experience is union of the soul with its spirit. . . .'

' "The Group have endeavoured to drop suggestions into your unconscious or subliminal mind, as you have been writing, and they are satisfied that you have been a successful intermediary."

In a postscript to this interesting communication, which I thought was possibly a little more critical than usual – a feature which surprised me a little in the light of his unvarying tolerance of other religions – he gives a clue to this.

"P.S. One of my previous lives was spent in India. Hence my criticism may seem in this letter somewhat over-critical of Indian philosophy. But in that previous life I saw too much of tragedy, partly because the finest men retreated from life instead of endeavouring to serve the people in the awful conditions prevalent there during that incarnation of mine. Seeking in the contemplative life their personal salvation, they displayed a neglect of the primary and fundamental virtue of loving one's neighbour. I warmly therefore appreciate your own treatment of Love in your book. It is of the Divine. To neglect the practice of love in service to others, is to neglect the highest attribute of God. However sinless the life of the ascetic Indian sage living in solitude, this lack in love is a weakness that sometime has to be rectified during the journey of the pilgrim in Eternity."

The extracts which I have presented to the reader from scripts, have naturally enough been selected for their general interest, or the importance of their theme. The lighter human touches were in the more personal parts of these scripts, and perhaps I may give one example. I had referred in my letter to the fact that he would be doubtless amused to know that I did a bit of oil-painting as a relaxation. In a postscript to one of the scripts he wrote:

"Your account of your painting as a relaxation charms me and makes me long to be back with you and compete in a daubers' tourney – the prize to be awarded to the most execrable daub of the lot, entered for the competition. The penalty for the loser is to hang that daub in his sitting-room, from which by fondly gazing at it daily, he may learn much – at any rate, how NOT to paint. I would certainly win the prize!"

The development of this humorous thought impressed me as very characteristic of my old friend.

I shall quote a substantial part of one last script dated January 27th, 1960. I had in my letters to him referred to mystical experience on several occasions. It was a topic much in my mind by reason of the book which I had written on this theme.[1] Ambrose returned to the subject in this script, in an effort to convey through words some idea of what higher forms of mystical experience implied.

[1] *Watcher on the Hills* (Hodder & Stoughton Ltd., 1959).

"Dear Raynor,

"I shall, to begin my story, first refer to a passage in *Watcher on the Hills*. It is in effect, 'Seeking a central rest undisturbed by the activities of the cosmos and its innumerable beings.' That was the mystical goal of the brave hard-pressed woman you tell of in your book. It is man's highest goal. He may not go further unless his is a very exceptional soul, as long as he is in the physical body. The term 'central rest' might cover most of the experiences of the mystical state known to men and women. In this Hither World neither could I proceed further than 'central rest' until I had had in the after-death, manifold experiences, yet my subtle body did not imprison me as in the flesh.

"I may say that it is only recently I passed beyond that human-mystical state which previously was my highest achievement. But the difference between central rest and the loftier condition is one, to put it crudely between play and work.

"The difference is infinite living, an activity indescribable which is the opposite of rest, and the supreme joy gained only by its product and the process of creativity. It is of course in its essence divine consciring – playing my part in the higher Imaginal as the spectator of a mighty drama, beholding an inconceivable vastness of experience and at the same time pin-pointing as it were: that is to say, creatively consciring in some tiny role in connection with some segment of the material universe; perhaps in an infinitely minute sense directing in unison with others the forces towards what Fawcett called Novelty. Novelty, as he means it, is progress – a leap forward – or as it mostly was in my case, the lesser task of maintaining the content already created.

"In any case, during these mystical experiences of exalted activity, my little unit blended with the Spirit of my Group-soul. I cannot express in words the ecstasy of this two-fold being and living in the state of high creativity, one's self a unit and yet the whole. But as no man may remain for long on one of the tallest of earth's mountain peaks, so I, a still crude being, have to fall back into the central rest, and from there lower and lower still, entering finally the habitation of the subtle body. To use a mundane analogy, it might be likened to going down in a lift from floor to floor, and for me the ground floor means association again with my subtle body. Yet my subtle body is so fine you could no more perceive it visually than you perceive the sea breezes as you meditate on some Australian shore during your holiday. But I assure you that on several occasions, I have had, after immense preparatory effort, the mystical experience of divine creativity while blended with and enclosed within the Spirit of the Group-soul. The bliss of such soaring, such inimitable activity defeats all speech or language. On those high levels, between our units, ourselves, there is neither speech nor language, but there is communion of a clarity that rhetoric, poetry of the noblest and most enlightening cannot express, for we are near then to the heart of the Mystery.

"You must understand, dear Raynor, that the wayfarer Ambrose still remains within the orbit of the planet Earth while in form, while inhabiting his subtle body. It is partly for the following reason. A few of my Group-soul and fewer still of those dear and intimate mortals who were in the design of my past earthly life are still living in the physical body. I must be there to greet them and aid them in their development after their demise. So my routine life is at present passed within the radius of earth, but my outward form vibrates at a different rate, on a different scale to that continuum of energy called the universe.

"Now Myers defined the subtle body as the old disguise, as it is in the likeness of himself when he was a man on earth. But at the time of your death I might be exploring, living temporarily at the even more advanced rate in another different scale. Then you would not be able to make contact with me. Nevertheless hearing your call sent out on the wings of thought to me, I would descend and adopt the old disguise. Thereby I could be with you on your new post-mortem level, and to you recognisable because I was in the old disguise. I would be in the familiar likeness of my self that you knew so well on earth.

"The ancient term 'the Body of Light' might describe the appearance of those souls I have encountered who dwell on the higher levels of energy when they work within an imaginal consciring, i.e. creatively imagining in relation to the life of the universe, each soul helping to maintain and conserve the exquisite balance of Nature in all its parts."

.   .   .

"You write, 'I wonder why you say, "There are certain sublime experiences we may not seek to communicate to anyone still living within terrestrial boundaries. The limitations of these boundaries are considered necessary in order that the design of the individual life be worked out." ' Then your comment, 'I cannot think it would make for dissatisfaction with earthly life leading to withdrawal from it. Should it not make for wonder, thanksgiving, and inspiration to appreciate that the goodness of God is so great?'

"Here is my reply. For karma, for reasons created by his past lives anterior to this earth life, a man has unconsciously created the design, generally speaking, of his Fate during his present earthly existence. The kind of temptations, difficulties, etc., are in the big events already there before him. Will he overcome them or will he fail? He has freewill, the power to choose. But Raynor, my dear fellow, if you had it your way you would load the dice. There is, in other words, interference with the design of the life of a religious or mystically-minded man if he is buoyed up by 'wonder, thanksgiving and inspiration' through learning of those sublime experiences, those higher mystical states. In order to make progress, in order that his self may grow, the religious man or mystic has to struggle, suffer pain, perhaps lose faith, perhaps, oh horror, be lost in the Dark Night of the Soul. There can be no short cuts for him. While he is on earth a certain limitation has to be his lot.

"Incidentally I may remind you that when on the Cross, Christ the Son of God cried out, 'My God, my God, why hast Thou forsaken me?' Why did God the loving Father permit His Son to be driven to the depths of such despair? Why in that awful hour did He not buoy Christ up, preserve his lost faith, by holding before him the vision of his glorious resurrection? Would it not have carried him through in a state of wonder, thanksgiving, and inspiration – made it all easy? Yes, but then the crucifixion would not have been the supreme test it was, a test that through the centuries since has shown the Christian how the Son of Man failed and yet the God within that Son of Man eventually succeeded despite that despairing cry.

"But to return to the mystic or religiously minded man I mentioned previously. Later on, if he has successfully overcome his trials and his supreme test, he will, on reaching supernal realities be far better qualified to realise the sublime experiences – and this because of the growth of his soul. But it grew through doubt, pain, through the hard way, through experience of despair. If the way had been made easy by certain knowledge of the mystical glory, such growth would not have occurred. . . ."

I wonder what impression these scripts per Miss Cummins' automatic writing, have made on my reader? When I consider and weigh the various possible theories, I am bound to say frankly that I am driven to the conviction that my old friend Ambrose Pratt, whom Miss Cummins had not met, and of whom she knew nothing (to the best of my knowledge), was indeed in communication with me. They bear all the marks of his first class mind, his critical approach, his wide knowledge, some of his deepest interests, and particularly in the more personal parts (which I have not quoted) his old friendship. He may have been wearing what he called "the old disguise" to communicate in this way, but the old disguise had outstanding qualities!

In one of my letters to him, I asked if the desire which he had expressed to me in the closing years of his life here – that he need not return to earth – had been granted. He told me that it had mercifully been granted to him. He urged me in several of his communications to express as persuasively and convincingly as possible in this age of scientific materialism, my conviction that life goes on after death. I have tried to do this elsewhere, and I hope that what I have disclosed in this essay will help others to the same conviction as it led me. I might fittingly conclude by quoting a fragment from one of the scripts. "Frederic Myers has recently said that his words written when on earth still remain true to him, 'The state of the departed souls is one of endless evolution in wisdom and love. Their loves of earth persist, and most of all those highest loves which seek their outlet in adoration and worship.'"